Keepe
Prophet's Sword

Joseph Bates Noble
Body Guard to the Prophet
Joseph Smith
1810 - 1900

By: Howard Carlos Smith

PREFACE

A few weeks ago while visiting my cousin I was given the opportunity, for the first time, to see the legion sword of the Prophet Joseph Smith. Holding the sword, I felt a spirit like I've never felt before almost like holding hands with the prophet himself.

This legion sword has been hidden away for 165 years and not to be on display. It has been handed down from father to son in the Noble family for a special purpose in giving testimony to Joseph Bates Noble a defender and bodyguard to the prophet. This is his story.

ACKNOWLEDGEMENTS

This book would not have been possible without the support of my wife, Jolene who patiently assisted me in editing and the transcription of these writings.

I'm also greatly indebted to the Noble family, especially my cousin Lamar and his wife Teri.

I also acknowledge my grandmother, Edith Adams Smith, for instilling within me as a young man the desire to carry on her work as a family researcher. We spent many hours with each other.

I would also like to thank the Daughters of the Utah Pioneers Museum and the Noble family for providing the pictures in this book.

Also, thanks to Lorin Robbins at Blip Color in designing the book cover and relic picture development.

Table of Contents

"WHY ME LORD?"

Joseph Bates Noble more than likely asked, "Why me, Lord?" as he hid away the prophet Joseph Smith's Nauvoo Legion sword. A casket cane would soon be a stow-away and the two relics would soon start a long journey into time. Comparable, it's almost like a large brown bear in hibernation spending the winter months in a dark cave only to awaken in the early spring.

The time for awakening is now and the winter has past. The year is 2009, spring is here, and the relics have spent 165 years in hiding. The two companions are like a very bright light sending understanding into the passages of time and each having a message to share.

The "Keeper of the Prophet's Sword" and "Casket Cane" is about pioneer Joseph Bates Noble. Who is this man named 'Joseph Bates Noble', and why is his name somewhat missing in the history books of the church? Let's take a look into his life.

Bates shares a little, "I am the son of Ezekiel Noble. My father was born in May, about the year 1785. My mother's maiden name was Theodosia Bates. Her father's name was Joseph Bates. My parents were married about the year 1805, and in 1815 moved to the state of New York, Penfield, Monroe County. I was born in 1810, January 14, and when at the age of five years, my father moved to the above mentioned place, where we lived until 1830. During this time my father's family had increased until we numbered eleven in family."[1]

Bates and Joseph Smith share the same first name – Joseph. Each started out as New Englanders by birth. Bates was born in Egremont, Massachusetts and Joseph came into the world on December 23, 1805. The Prophet being five years older was like an older brother to Bates. Their birth houses were only a few miles apart.

Bates continues, "When at the age of fourteen, my father, having a large family, and not much to help himself with, depended upon the labor of his own hands for the support of so large a family. I went to work by the month for Nelson Fullom for six months at $5.00 per month. I, with part of my summer's work, bought a cow for my father and the remainder I clothed myself with, and from this time on till I was eighteen years of age I was from home most of the time."[2]

Bates mentions that at age eighteen he went to live with one Harrison A. Fairchild, to learn to be a miller (or to tend mill). He learned the miller trade and at age nineteen moved on to another job working for a Mr. Tomlinson.

He states, "I will say here that I became acquainted with a man by the name of Eben Wilcox while I was in the employ of Mr. Fairchild, and went to work for Mr. Tomlinson. Eben Wilcox had the oversight of the mill as a Miller. The mill was conveyed into other hands at the first part of the year. Mr. Wilcox and myself went to Avon, Livingston County, and hired to Mr. McMillen to tend mill. Mr. Wilcox earned $26 per month. I got $18 per month".[3]

At age twenty, Bates stood at 5 feet 8 inches tall weighing somewhere around 165 pounds. He was strong, had trimmed hair, sometimes clean shaven and other times sporting an under chin beard. He knew how to mount and ride a spirited horse, shoe a horse, use a sword, fire a pistol with great accuracy, and hunt game with a Ball and Cap musket never missing the mark.[4]

"I continued to work at the milling business. Sometime in the Fall of 1832, I heard for the first time the gospel preached by Brigham and Joseph Young, and Heber C. Kimball. I said in my heart, "that is truth according to the spirit that is in me, for I was a person who thought much about the things of God, and often mediated and wondered in my heart, and asked myself this question: Where is the people of God? Where are they that exercised the faith before Him that our father's did? I have, from the age of twelve years old, often felt after the God of my fathers, and have from time to time obtained by the whispering of this spirit a testimony of my acceptance with him. I have a proud heart, and from the good intention I gave from what was put into my care I gained the confidence of all. I took time in endeavoring to excel and minding my own business."

"I was baptized in the fall of 1832, as also was Eben Wilcox, and some four or five others, who bore our testimony in favor of the work of God, that he had commenced in these last days by revealing to his servant, Joseph Smith, the keys of the Holy Priesthood, authorizing him to build up His kingdom on the earth."[5]

Bates Noble with a testimony of the gospel made preparations to travel 200 miles to meet the modern day prophet. The rough journey was made by foot and horse. No written material covering this journey, nevertheless, he was an expert on a horse. He arrived in Kirtland crossing paths with Joseph Smith.

Joseph was working the hayfields this day on his 140 acre farm. The new convert, Bates, was won by his humanness and informality. The prophet's countenance was that of a plain, honest man, full of benevolence and void of deceit. He was a tall, powerful, altogether striking figure. Joseph Smith's four brothers were also tall, well-formed men, all six feet or over, and together with their father they formed an arresting picture as they walked about the Kirtland streets.

That early summer morning Bates walked the hayfields to meet the Prophet. Joseph Smith invited him to stack hay, this being no easy task. Both men were physically strong, hard workers, with personalities to which anyone would enjoy being in their presence. Stories were shared as the hay was pitched into the horse driven wagon. One day turned into a week bonding friendship with many strands to be woven into a friendship

lasting a lifetime and throughout eternity. It was a very interesting week one-on-one with the Prophet giving testimony as to the truthfulness of the new gospel. He shared stories of visiting angels and much more.

Several books could be written about Bates Noble even though this is not my intention. Nevertheless, I would like to share a quick resume of several accomplishments about his life in general:

- Helped support his father's family.
- At age 22 baptized by Brigham Young.
- Stayed nine days at Joseph and Emma Smith's house. Pitched hay seven days with Joseph and Hyrum Smith.
- Answered a call to serve in Zion's Camp.
- Mary Adeline Beman was the love of his life. Nine children – six died before age eight.
- Bishop of the Kirtland Ward.
- Member of the First Quorum of Seventy.
- Attended the School of the Prophets.
- Learned several languages including Hebrew.

- Witnessed heavenly manifestations in the Kirtland Temple.
- Head bodyguard to the Prophet.
- Messenger for Joseph Smith.
- Several visits with the Prophet at Liberty Jail.
- Missionary in southern Ohio.
- Healed by the Prophet's hand.
- Nauvoo 5th Ward Bishop.
- President Smith's family attended his ward.
- 1841 he performed the first plural marriage in the Church.
- Held the rank of Major in the Nauvoo Legion.
- Keeper of "The Prophet's Nauvoo Legion Sword".
- Keeper of "The Oak Casket Cane".
- Key officer in rescuing the bodies.
- Led a company of 171 pioneers into the Salt Lake Valley.
- Built the first adobe house in West Bountiful, Utah.
- Married Sylvia Loretta Mecham in January 1857 and she shared in building the new house. Large family.
- Years later he served on the High Council, was a Stake Patriarch and a Bishop of the West Bountiful First Ward.
- Served several missions - one to England.[6]

Yes, this list could go on and on and on. Nevertheless, it gives the reader a feel to the sort of man Joseph Bates Noble is and was during his mortal span of ninety years. He never once turned his back to God or his friend Joseph Smith the Latter Day Mormon Prophet.

NOTES:

1. Autobiography of Joseph Bates Noble, Typescript, BYU-S, p.1.

2. Ibid, p.1.

3. Ibid, p.1.

4. Description given by Lamar Noble, great-grandson to Joseph Bates Noble.

5. Autobiography of Joseph Bates Noble, Transcript, BYU-S, p.2.

6. West Bountiful 1848-1988, "A Pictorial History" by LaRue Hugoe and Edith Deppe, pp. 21-23. Also overview given by Lamar Noble – great-grandson to Joseph Bates Noble.

A SWORD FIT
FOR A PROPHET

Never before has anyone viewed pictures showing Joseph Smith's Legion Sword. These pictures are the first and it has a story to tell so here we go. The Prophet's sword is of a unique design and molded with quality from the maker and designed for a man of large stature. The sword will speak out giving you clues.

You may ask, was the sword made out of gold and silver. For comparison let's look at the Sword of Laban as described by Nephi in the Book of Mormon. The time schedule is in the city of Jerusalem about six hundred years before the birth of Jesus Christ. Nephi speaks, "And I beheld his sword, and I drew it forth from the sheath thereof; and the hilt thereof was of pure gold, and the workmanship thereof was exceedingly fine, and I saw that the blade thereof was of the most precious steel."[1]

I was privileged in November-December 2007 of being temporary care keeper to the sacred sword belonging to Joseph Smith. It was a

choice experience and I spent many hours studying the Legion Sword regarding its measurements, photo taking, and getting a feel as to the hilt of the sword. The sword provided a peaceful spirit within our home.

The Prophet's sword is not made of pure gold nor is the blade of most precious steel. The hilt has a metal protector of black steel giving the appearance of being interlaced or I could say being intertwined with three distinct hand protectors. The hand protector is very

MAJOR GEN. JOSEPH SMITH,
Mormon Prophet.

Joseph Smith

prominent projecting like fingers around the hand to one holding the sword.

There is only one painting of Lt. General Joseph Smith in Nauvoo Legion Uniform standing and posing for this portrait. This was painted by Sutcliffe Maudsley during the Nauvoo days. He drew a profile portrait of the Prophet to be used on a map of the city. Little did the thirty-three year old Maudsley know that Joseph's likeness would someday become one of just a handful of original images of the Prophet and would create a place in history for him as an artist. Joseph Smith signed the original portrait.[2]

Maudsley's original portrait portrays an artist having a difficult time in describing the three metal fingers protruding around the right hand of Joseph Smith while gripping the hilt of the sword. The blade is pointing downward and it almost looks like the Prophet has three distorted fingers. To distinguish the black steel metal protector, he placed a gold ring band around Joseph's ring finger. As I mentioned the Legion Sword is very different especially the hilt and would pose a problem to an amateur artist.

Maudsley as a young boy demonstrated some talent in drawing and was "bound out" to learn art. He later became a skilled calico pattern maker and designer in the textile mills. In addition, by the time he emigrated to Nauvoo, he must have also learned the basic elements of profile portrait drawing.[3]

Maudsley made one portrait profile showing Hyrum and Joseph Smith as brothers standing tall sideways in Sunday dress. Joseph appears to be approximately one inch taller than Hyrum and larger through the chest, arms and legs. Joseph is definitely more robust in this engraving than his brother.

As the writer and temporary care keeper of the Prophet's sword, I stand tall at six feet. Placing the sheath sword to my left side and using my right hand to draw the sword, I'm not tall enough to draw the sword from the sheath. The sword blade measures 35-1/2 inches, and the hilt handle measures 5-1/2 inches and the overall length is 41 inches. Let's get a better perspective and refer to the picture showing the sword compared to a household step ladder. The picture tells it all – the prophet was a tall man.

Joseph Smith's sword is approximately 175 years old. The sword was given to him by

his friend Wilford Woodruff in early 1834.[4] The Prophet carried the sword during the long march to Zion's Camp. Also around this same time a somewhat humorous report was written by Eber D. Howe in the Painesville Telegraph's May 9, 1834 issue. It stated, "The prophet, it is said, has a sword over four feet long." He also likens Joseph Smith to "Peter the Hermit", in the days of the crusader.[5]

The overall condition considering its age is excellent and the leather strap, sheath, hilt and sword blade show little wear. The sword has been hidden away since June 1844. It was passed from father-to-son, father-to-son, and father-to-son. Lamar Noble great-grandson to Joseph Bates Noble is now the "Keeper of the Prophet's Sword".[6]

How tall a man was Joseph Smith? First let's take a look at Father Smith, he was a large man, ordinarily weighing two hundred pounds;

he was six feet two inches in height, and well proportioned, strong and active.[7] Joseph Fielding Smith states that "Don Carlos Smith, the youngest brother of the Prophet, was six feet four inches tall, very straight, strong and active".[8]

In researching most people suggest that the Prophet was somewhere around six feet tall, strong and well built. Other's say he was just tall and gives no indication as to his height. For example, Parley P. Pratt states the following description: "President Smith was in person tall and well built, strong and active; of a light complexion, light hair, blue eyes, very little beard, and of an expression peculiar to himself, on whom the eyes naturally rested with interest, and was never weary of beholding."[9]

In the History of Illinois, Governor Ford stated, "He was a full six feet high, strongly built, and uncommonly well muscled."[10]

From study, measurements and handling the sword I feel quite confident making the following statement. Keep in mind that Don Carlos Smith stood at six feet four inches, and Joseph Smith, Sr. stood at six foot two inches.

"Joseph Smith the Latter Day Prophet stood bare foot six foot three inches tall and six foot four inches in his boots. His brother Hyrum stood at six foot two inches tall. Give or take – Hyrum's weight was two hundred thirty pounds and Joseph's weight was two hundred forty-five pounds. One may say the Smith men were well built, muscular and tall. A modern day football coach for the NFL would be more than happy to sign them up on the team".[11]

Joseph Smith was a wrestling prowess. No one could throw him in the ring. October 1838 he was energetically preparing Far West for a siege. Walking around town he came upon a group of disconsolate guards shivering around some small firebrands. The men were gloomy faced and so he caught the first one and then another by the shoulder, shaking them roughly. "Get out of here and wrestle, run, jump, do anything but mope around, warm yourselves up." The prophet challenged them to wrestle. Catching his spirit, the men one-by-one stepped into the ring to try their strength, while the others shouted and applauded. Not one could throw Joseph, and finally, laughing in fun and sweating, he left the ring to make way for a lesser man.[12]

Bates Noble was also very athletic – he often told of wrestling with the Prophet and indulging in many other activities with him. He once excelled in a contest when he carried a barrel of flour up eighteen flights of stairs. He loved to do step dancing in the early days. Later in life, at the age of seventy-five, he was once in a farm wagon. He stepped on the hind wheel of the wagon and jumped lightly down then went skipping away. He said to his sons, "Well, boys, if you can do that when you are seventy-five you'll do very well".[13]

A strand of Joseph's hair can be viewed in an unusual picture entitled the "Hair Tree Picture". It is located on the first floor of the Daughters of the Utah Pioneers Memorial Museum. The willow tree displays thirty nine branches each with a different strand of hair. Brigham Young, John Taylor and other prominent members of the Church make up the branches. Joseph Smith's hair is a mixture of blonde and light brown.

The "Hair Tree Picture" was fashioned by Harriet Critchlow Jensen. During the early years it was displayed within the main entrance of the Salt Lake Temple. In 1967 the temple underwent remodeling and the picture was donated to the museum.[14]

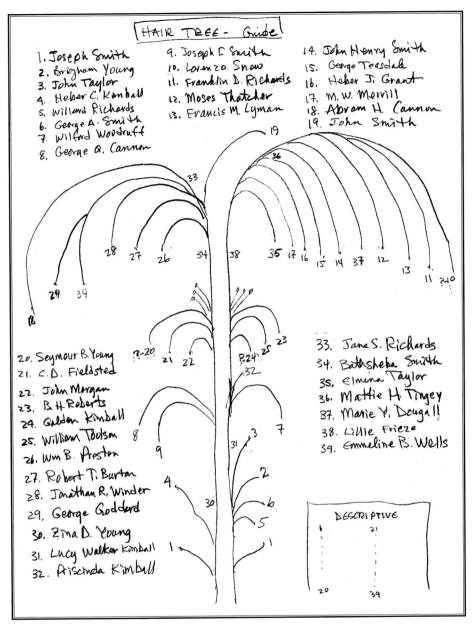

HAIR TREE - Guide

1. Joseph Smith
2. Brigham Young
3. John Taylor
4. Heber C. Kimball
5. Willard Richards
6. George A. Smith
7. Wilford Woodruff
8. George Q. Cannon

9. Joseph F. Smith
10. Lorenzo Snow
11. Franklin D. Richards
12. Moses Thatcher
13. Francis M. Lyman

14. John Henry Smith
15. George Teasdale
16. Heber J. Grant
17. M. W. Merrill
18. Abram H. Cannon
19. John Smith

20. Seymour B. Young
21. C. D. Fieldsted
22. John Morgan
23. B. H. Roberts
24. Golden Kimball
25. William Toolson
26. Wm B. Preston
27. Robert T. Burton
28. Jonathan R. Winder
29. George Goddard
30. Zina D. Young
31. Lucy Walker Kimball
32. Priscinda Kimball

33. Jane S. Richards
34. Bathsheba Smith
35. Elmina Taylor
36. Mattie H. Tingey
37. Marie Y. Dougall
38. Lillie Frieze
39. Emmeline B. Wells

DESCRIPTIVE

In the "Church News", week ending March 22, 2008, a statement regarding a photo image of Joseph Smith stated "A purported image of Joseph Smith is circulating widely on the Internet. Some persons have mistakenly claimed that this image belongs to the Church of Jesus Christ of Latter Day Saints, and that Church officials have verified or are verifying its authenticity. These claims are not true".[15]

It goes on to say with the "basis of available evidence it is not possible to confirm that the image is, in fact, of Joseph Smith".[16]

It mentions that the Church does not have or own this photograph or any image of Joseph Smith other than several early artists' portrayals of him. Nevertheless it states, "The Church does have the death mask of Joseph Smith."[17]

After viewing the death mask[18], I feel very confident in stating: Joseph Smith the Latter Day Prophet was indeed a very large man in stature, and strong in strength. Joseph was of light complexion, light hair, blue eyes, and very little beard. He definitely does not reflect the image recently placed on the Internet.

NOTES:

1. Book of Mormon 1 Nephi 4:9

2. www.lds.org/Museum/exhibits/maudsley/home/1,13480,4088-1-3,00.html.

    www.rickgrunder.com/Books%20for%20Sale/BennettExpose/bennett.htm.

3. Ibid, refer to note # 2.

4. "Woodruff and Zion's Camp", by Alexander, p. 137.

5. "Joseph Smith – Rough Stone Rolling", by Richard Lyman Bushman, Vintage Books, 1st edition, 2007, p. 238, also p. 610 under note # 27.

6. Lamar Noble – great-grandson to J.B. Noble, Keeper of Joseph Smith's legion sword, also casket cane, and Ball and Cap musket rifle belonging to Joseph Bates Noble. Present time is 2008.

7. Comprehensive History of the Church by B.H. Roberts, Vol. II, 1965, p. 41.

8. Essentials in Church History by Joseph Fielding Smith, 16th Edition, 1960, p.311.

9. Autobiography of Parley P. Pratt, pp. 47-48.

10. History of Illinois, Governor Ford's Stmt., p. 335.

11. Statement made by Howard Carlos Smith, Author of this book, after much research in studying the legion sword belonging to Joseph Smith.

12. No Man Knows My History – by Fawn M. Brodie, 2nd Edition 1962, p. 235.

13. Journal History, Historical Record, Vols. 5,6,7,8, Noble Genealogy. Biographical Books and Family Traditions.

14. Picture approximately 18 x 26 inside white ornate frame with gold liner that is a branching willow tree whose branches are made of hair attributed to early leaders of the LDS church. Made by Harriet Critchlow Jensen and presented to the Salt Lake Temple, where it hung in the main entrance until it was remodeled. At the bottom right is placed a "DESCRIPTIVE" card that is a numeric legend matching labels on the strands of hair, 1 thru 39. The legend is reproduced with ART0051a graphic. This note accompanied the picture graphic provided by DUP Museum.

15. Church News, week ending March 22, 2008, Vol. 78, No. 12, Title: Church explains claims regarding photo image of Joseph Smith, p.2.

16. Ibid, p.2.

17. Ibid. p.2.

18. Death mask of Joseph Smith, view picture. No Man Knows My History, by Fawn M. Brodie, 2nd Edition, 1962, p.394.

BATES NOBLE JOINS THE MARCH

3

On 24 February 1834, the Lord revealed to Joseph Smith that he should organize a group of men to march from Kirtland to Missouri and help restore the saints to their lands. The Lord promised that His presence would go with them and that "all victory and glory" would be brought to pass through their "diligence, faithfulness, and prayers of faith"[1]. Bates Noble was asked to join the march.

One may ask why the Prophet would authorize this army? It was to protect the God given rights to all Latter Day Saints living in the state of Missouri. State authorities converted men into mobs allowing them to plunder the saints, burn their houses and lay waste the land. They compelled families to sign away their properties and leaving them no choice but to leave the state. To resist the militia mob was to be guilty of treason against the State of Missouri.

Plans were made for an army of five hundred men, however after recruiting the yield was fewer than two hundred men.[2] All the households in Kirtland chipped in by providing old muskets, rifles, pistols and trusty swords. These were soon put into a state of repair and scoured up. Some were borrowed while others were manufactured by their own mechanics.[3]

Bates Noble speaks, "In the spring of 1834, I settled up my business because there was a proclamation made by the servants of God that the strength of His house was wanted to go up to Missouri to redeem Zion, (or for the redemption of Zion). I accordingly volunteered, bid farewell to my father's family and all my acquaintances for a season, and started on the first day of May. I arrived in Kirtland on the sixth, found the company had left, that they were to be in Wooster that night, a distance of 50 miles. I hired Brother Johnson to take me with a horse and buggy to Wooster that night, which he did. We arrived there about 9:00 in the evening. I called up a public house and I found by inquiring that there was a company of Mormons who came in there that evening on their way to Missouri. My heart leaped for joy. I went to where they were. They were glad to see me, especially Elder Eben Wilcox. They began to fear that something had happened to me. I was some behind the time appointed."[4]

"About two days from Wooster we overtook the rest of our company. We numbered 205 in all, and we organized ourselves into companies of tens and fifties and hundreds, with captains over them, and a baggage wagon for each ten. We received much good instruction from President Joseph Smith from time to time as circumstances would permit. We traveled the more part of the way through an old settled country. Considerable excitement prevailed. Many questions were asked with regard to our motives, what we intended to do. We answered them as we thought best, or as we were instructed from time to time. President Smith would have us travel sometimes with arms on and sometimes without it. Sometimes most of us were in our own wagons, and then sometimes we were all out. We did not travel on Sundays. We stopped and held meetings. When we were near a village or town we would give notice for meetings. Sometimes we would have a Methodist preaching, Presbyterians and Universalist, and sometimes all in one day. We could easily make them believe or think that the company was made up of these different denominations and at the same time teach some of the items of our faith by such persons as had previously belonged to these different sects. They can give it the proper tone."[5]

Let's touch on one incident Bates witnessed in making his way across Indiana. A large snake is sunning in the middle of a dirt road. Martin Harris offered his naked toe to a five foot black snake in the road and when it refused to bite him proclaimed an apostolic victory over the serpent. However, when he repeated the experiment with another snake he got a severe bite on the ankle. The company jeered uproariously at his lack of faith, and Joseph publicly upbraided him for making a mockery of the Lord's gifts.[6]

Crossing Illinois, Bates also witnessed a super natural occurrence. Zion's company stopped by an Indian mound near the Illinois River and Joseph excavated a human skeleton from the mounts surface. The eyes were upon the prophet. President Smith speaks, "This man in mortal life was a Lamanite. He was a large, thick-set man, and a man of God. His name was Zelph. He was a warrior and chieftain under the great Prophet Onandagus. This great prophet was known from the eastern sea to the Rocky Mountains". Lifting the thigh bone which had been broken, Joseph pointed to an arrowhead still lodged between the ribs. Joseph then described in vivid detail the great battle to which Zelph had been killed. The bones were then placed back into the mound and covered with earth in honor to this great Indian. The arrowhead was kept as a souvenir by Brigham Young and as a testimony to this great warrior and chieftain.[7]

Bates continues, "We were often countered by men on horseback and at ferries where one would think they need not mistake who it was. I never heard of our being numbered less than twice our actual number. Reports said we were a thousand strong. I have somewhere among my papers a brief sketch of places and distances, and of things that transpired on the way, which I intended to put in this journal, for there were many things said and done that to me were interesting and no doubt would be to my friends."

Making their way into Missouri the heat became very intense and Bates was suffering from blistered feet along with others. When it rained the dirt road became quagmires and he found it hard to walk in without feeling stuck. The supply wagons at times were stuck in every mud hole and frequently broke down altogether.[8]

Soon the soldiers headed west on the north side of the mighty Missouri River advancing slowly over the prairies until on June 18th they pitched their tents one mile from the outskirts of Richmond. The next morning Zion's Army passed through the town and towards evening they camped on an elevated piece of ground between two branches of Fishing River. Unbeknownst the enemy devised a plan to do battle at Fishing River. Bates Noble was officially called to be a bodyguard to the Prophet. There was a sense in camp that something was about to happen.[9]

Why the bodyguards? James Campbell, an enemy to the church and leader of a group thirsting for the blood of the Prophet, vowed that he would intercept Joseph and Zion's Army before he reached any of his colonists. He stated, "The eagles and turkey buzzards shall eat my flesh" and swore to fixing Joe Smith and his army so that their skin would not hold shucks before two days are past."[10]

Choosing eleven lieutenants, James started after sunset on June 19 crossing the treacherous Missouri River to secretly ambush and murder the prophet. It was not Joseph Smith's time and the Lord had other plans in store. Halfway across the swollen river, the boat capsized and the men were swimming for their lives. Bates noted in his journal that one man floated down stream to a river island from which he swam off naked about daylight, borrowed a mantle to hide his shame, and slipped home rather shy of the vengeance of God.

The majority of the river party was not so lucky. Seven of the twelve men drowned, including their leader James Campbell whose body floated down stream and lodged upon a pile of driftwood. There the body was found three weeks later. The flesh picked clean. Isn't it interesting that James predicted that "the eagles and turkey buzzards shall eat my flesh". Mr. Campbell had fulfilled his oath with his own flesh.

Next, another attack was planned against the 'Army of the Lord'. Learning that Zion's Camp planned to stay at Fishing River, around 200 men gathered at Williams Ferry on June 20 and prepared to cross the Missouri River for the attack. They were armed and prepared to take out the Lord's Army.

The first scow load of forty men had scarcely left the landing when a squall broke upon the river. "Wind and rain, hail and thunder met them in great wrath and soon softened their direful courage and frustrated all their designs". The mandate of vengeance had gone forth from the "God of Battles" to protect his servants from the destruction from their enemies.[11]

The boat was successful in crossing the river and the occupants opened fire while they were still some distance from the Mormon camp. A cold morning mist was coming off the swollen raging torrent and rain soaked their ammunition. Vicious hail drops from the sky above drove them into shanties and hollow trees for cover and shelter. The earth trembled and quaked. One man was killed by lightning and another had his hand torn off by a fractious horse. The men on the other side of the Missouri River gave up their forty comrades as lost and they themselves crawled like cowards under their wagons to escape this hail blast and storm. The surprise attack was to no avail upon the "Lord's Army".[12]

A portion of Zion's Camp had found shelter from the vicious storm in a Baptist Church. Joseph Smith was in and out repeatedly checking reports from his scouts, for the rifle shots had warned him of the coming trouble.[13]

Joseph satisfied as to the failure of the planned attack upon his men spent the remainder of night in rest. The Prophet shaking the water from his hat and clothes declared soberly: "Boys, there is some meaning to this, God is in this storm". The rain and hail had dampened the ardor as well as the ammunition of the attackers. The next morning the forty who had previously crossed the swollen river rowed back in shame to gather with their army and returned to Independence to join up with others.[14]

Two days after this planned attack Cornelius Gilliam, Sheriff of Clay County, came to Zion's Camp to meet with Joseph Smith. Cornelius is one who campaigned for Sheriff with the slogan that he had shot more wolves than any other man in Missouri and he minced no words to enter Jackson County with arms would be an act of insurrection.

Sheriff Cornelius went on to say that the Governor had said explicitly that he would bring his state militia down upon the heads of these invaders. To remain camped near the borders was to invite bloodshed. What he did not say was that the Mormons and their families were already attacked, their houses burned, the people driven from their personal property, the plundering of their farm animals and gardens and the burning of their farms. These people were left out into the cold of night and the 'Army of the Lord' was there to secure their rights as citizens in a new world and free country.[15]

The Prophet and men only had two alternatives; one was to sell their lands, disperse their army and return to Kirtland, or to purchase the land of the old settlers at double its price and value. It was a no lose situation.

Joseph Smith, after hearing the Sheriff out, made a promise that Zion's Camp would not cross the Missouri River and into Jackson County. It was a peace plan given by Joseph Smith to end the war.

The Mormons would be able to purchase all property of the settlers in Jackson County who were Mormon Baiters, the price to be set by twelve disinterested men and payment to be made within one year. The damages already sustained must be deducted from the value of the property. The damages were high, farms and homes of the Mormon pioneers had been burned to the ground leaving many of the families in the cold. Some had been beaten by the mobs and outright murdered.[16]

Several hours after the departure of the Sheriff, Joseph called his men together and read a new revelation commanding them to wait for a little season for the redemption of Zion. This revelation was given through Joseph Smith by the Lord on Fishing River, Missouri the 22nd day of June 1834. The full revelation is recorded in Section 105 of the Doctrine and Covenants by the Church of Jesus Christ of Latter Day Saints.

To me verse 15 stands out in that the Lord said, *"Behold, the destroyer I have sent forth to destroy and lay waste mine enemies; and not many years hence they shall not be left to pollute mine heritage, and to blaspheme my name upon the lands which I have consecrated for the gathering together of my saints."*[17]

The revelation goes on to say that the men of the army had been brought to Missouri for "a trial of their faith", and now were to return to Kirtland, Ohio. Some of the Lord's Army shouted for action and was pacified only by a personal perusal of the revelation.

In the early morning hours of June 23rd, the expedition known as Zion's Army, breaks camp resuming its march along a circuitous course around the head of Fishing River, to avoid the deep water and making its way towards Clay County. Bates Noble's next stop would end at the head of Rush Creek. A test was about to fall upon him testing him to the utmost of his spirit. The trip so far was quite pleasant; nevertheless, something was amiss and about to come upon him and his fellow friends in arms.

NOTES:

1. D&C 103:36

2. Essentials in Church History by Joseph Fielding Smith, 16th Edition, 1960, pp. 170-171 and No Man Knows My History, by Fawn M. Brodie, 2nd Edition, 1962, p. 147.

3. E.D. Howe: Mormonism Unveiled, pp.155-6.

4. Journal of Joseph Bates Noble, Typescript, BYU-S, p. 3.

5. Ibid, p.3.

6. No Man Knows My History, by Fawn M. Brodie, 2nd Edition, 1962, p. 147.

7. Ibid, p. 149. Also, see Documentary History of the Church, Vol. 2:79, for this interesting incident!

8. Journal of Joseph Bates Noble, Typescript, BYU-S, p. 3.

9. Hyrum Smith, by Pearson H. Corbett; 1963, p. 127.

10. Early Days in Missouri, Letter 16.

11. Hyrum Smith, by Pearson H. Corbett; 1963, p. 131.

12. Essentials in Church History, by Joseph Fielding Smith, 1950, p. 174. Also, Joseph Smith, op. cit., Vol. II, pp. 103-105.

13. History of the Church, Vol. II, p. 104. This story was told by Wilford Woodruff.

14. No Man Knows My History, by Fawn M. Brodie, 2nd Edition, 1985, p. 155.

15. Journal of Joseph Bates Noble, Transcript, BYU-S, p. 3.

16. No Man Knows My History, by Fawn M. Brodie, 2nd Edition, 1985, p. 185.

17. D&C Section 105.

BODIES BURNED
ON RUSH HILL

Bates Noble states, "We arrived in Clay County Missouri, without the loss of any. The Lord blessed us in a wonderful manner. We could see and feel that His care was over us. By His might and power we were preserved. Many were taken sick on the way. They were administered to and soon well."[1]

When within five miles of Liberty, the party was met by General Atchison and others, advising the prophet that the citizens of Liberty were much enraged.[2]

Bates speaks up, "We told them they well knew that our people had been driven from Jackson County, and from their lands. They had bought up government land and paid cash for it. We had come to see the law put in force against those that had broken it, and to see our people reinstated onto their land. They acknowledged it was right. They should reinstate our people back onto their lands. These men pledged themselves to use all their influence to bring about this thing. They told us the whole country was very much excited. The Missourians were greatly upset hearing that we were 2000 strong, well armed with several pieces of artillery and that we intended to kill all, both great and small."[3]

In response to General Atchison's solicitation, the party turned its course, wheeling to the left, and crossing the prairie and woodland making its way to set camp on the bank of Rush Creek. It should be noted that Rush Creek heads about two miles northwest of Liberty and empties into the Missouri River seven miles southeast of Liberty.

Reaching Rush Creek, the men set up the camp quickly as directed by their prophet. Zion's Camp is on a slight hill somewhat open in an area with thick grass and encircled with trees extending to the river edge. Being near July, the day is hot, the flies are out, and some snakes linger near the river edge on this humid cloudy day.

Bates said, "While in this place, President Joseph Smith received the word of the Lord, saying our offering was accepted, comparative to that of Abraham. Our hearts rejoiced when we heard this. A few were for crossing the Missouri River into Jackson County or die trying. At this time there was stationed at the crossing 500 men. Some two weeks previous to this time President Smith told us plainly there was a scourge coming from the camp. He said he had prayed but nevertheless it will come."[4]

Following the order of the captains, Bates Noble and friend Eben Wilcox along with others set up their tents and supplies, neither having the slightest idea of what was about to come upon them. Bates continues, "We thought it would come from our enemies who were threatening us continually, but at the time when we were dismissed to make our own arrangements to get back, behold a cholera came on us with mighty power, and fourteen of our best men fell, and I myself, very narrowly escaped with my life."[5]

Where oh where did the deadly scourge come from? Think of marching through infested communities down with cholera and not knowing it. These men with Zion's Camp drank water from the rivers and accepted food and water from stops along the way. Catching cholera is like an eternity of suffering crowded into a few hours or short days of agony followed by a sudden crises of the disease and the victim never losses consciousness until the merciful end comes. The cholera toxin soon stops the heart of its victim.

Columbia University Medical Guide, 1985, page 522 states the following: *Nausea, vomiting, diarrhea, abdominal pains, cramps, and fever quickly lead to dehydration and can quickly travel to others. Food and water are the main contaminates with unsanitary conditions.*[6]

The word 'cholera' brought great fear upon Bates and all within this brave army. Was this to be their demise after traveling 1,000 long miles in making a final stop named Zion's Camp?

Three key steps to remember in regarding the scourge (1) the war was at an end, (2) the men were dismissed and free to make their way home, (3) suddenly the scourge came upon them with mighty power.

The war was over; nevertheless the men were still on guard for a surprise attack. Cholera broke out in the camp during the night of June 24. Charles C. Rich, officer of the camp guard, was concerned about being attacked by enemies during the night. "I thought there was an attack, some of the guards were seized with the cholera and dropped as if they had been shot." [7]

At this time if you were given a choice as to your final demise, what would you prefer? One, an unsheathe sword through your heart; two, a large lead ball passing through your body, or three, cholera? Zion's Army would definitely prefer the sword blade and the lead ball. This way you go out in style, honor, bravery, and somewhat have control over the situation and circumstances.

Soon others were seized upon violently with cholera. To them it was an unknown disease in the frontier of Missouri. The fear of spreading this disease was upon everyone's mind as they witnessed their comrades falling. Men were immediately asked to volunteer in caring of the sick. Bates stepped forward and held his right hand up. To volunteer, you put your life at risk and Bates put his life on the line along with others.

To some it was hard to believe what suddenly hit upon them. Bates was age 24, his friend Eben age 28, the prophet age 29, and almost all in their twenties, some in their early 30's, and several in their 40's. Zion's Camp was healthy, vigorous, strong, well armed, and ready for a fight. Now the men were dropping like flies. Sixty-eight men dropped in pain onto their backs unable to eat, drink, or hardly move their limbs. Some died quickly while others lingered for several days. Fourteen soldiers didn't return home.

The prophet acted quickly in separating the sick away from the healthy. The small one room tents were placed into small bands. The side canvas of each tent could either be opened or closed depending on the summer heat of day or night.

Bates set up his hospital tent and with the help of others carried four fallen soldiers and placed each upon a blanket onto the ground. His care keeping included his best friend Eben Wilcox. The Prophet Joseph Smith with others visited each tent, holding hands, making a ring around each and pronounced a Priesthood Blessing upon them. Some may ask, why not the anointing of oil and the laying on of hands? Why the ring around the receiving one? It was to control the spread of the disease. Those sick on the blankets were semi-covered with body fluids and near death.

Shortly after being a care keeper of the sick, Bates Noble fell to his knees with extreme pain and in his own words states, "I then, by the request of Brothers Young and Kimball, went with them to the house of Peter Whitmer, to the village of Liberty, about two miles distant from our last encampment. I there was violently seized with the cholera, puking and purging violently, then cramping from head to foot, in a most powerful manner, with a burning fever in my bowels. In this situation I lay forty hours. My voice and my hearing had nearly left me."

"While in this situation Brothers Brigham Young and Joseph Young, Heber C. Kimball, Orson Hyde, Peter Whitmer, with some three or four more prayed for me. While I was lying on the floor they formed a ring around me. While praying in this situation, the veil seemed very thin between me and my God, and I realized things that I never before thought of. Such were the blessings of God upon me that I nearly had an open vision. Through the faith of my brethren who was in exercise for me, I got up and with their assistance put on my clothes." [8]

Now back to the hospital tent, Bates' responsibility was to keep the fallen men cool and clean as possible with a wet cloth. Others assisted him allowing him a break and sleep. The first day of care his best friend Eben Wilcox died and by the weekend all four were dead. Bates in his journal had written, "It was my lot to assist in taking care of four of them in one small room until they were dead."[9] Some may say the small room was in a log house and some may say it was a four wall tent. Either answer is no avail, it makes no difference. As the writer, I prefer the tent to me it makes more sense as it is cholera and who would want to chance exposure to their family.

How to bury the remains is a searching question and some seem to lean this way, quoting the Newsletter #14 Jackson County, Missouri Summer 1997 – Title: Zion's Camp Monument, P. 2 [Martin Diary] "That night other bodies were carried on a horse sled to the bank of a small stream which empties into Rush Creek. Graves were dug in the dark, under torch light, to keep the fact of the presence of cholera from the knowledge of the inhabitants, and thus prevent, if possible, unnecessary excitement and trouble." (It also mentions that it appeared as if some of the bodies had been dead a week.)[10]

Bates Noble makes one bold statement in his journal, "This Brother Wilcox was one of four I mentioned of assisting in taking care of till they were burned." And he continues, "Never in my life did I feel to mourn like as on this occasion. I was sensible that a strong cord of friendship bound us together, but did not know that our hearts were so completely knit together as I found they were."[11]

The grave was dug and soon covered with soil. The burning prevented the dreaded cholera from spreading upon others.

Bates states, "I started back for the Ohio with Lyman Johnson, Sylvester Smith, Luke Johnson, Zebedee Coltren, and Aerubable Snow, and two or three others. Never had I experienced before such a manifestation of the blessings of God as at this time. I continued to gain strength very fast so that in six or seven days I could do my portion of walking, as we had but one baggage wagon. I would like to say here that President Joseph Smith and others strove with their might to rebuke the destroyer and continued to do it until the Lord told him to go away, and then he left, and not till then. We continued our march traveling twenty-five miles a day. We arrived in Kirtland the first day of August, and found President Joseph Smith had arrived a few days before us, all in tolerable good health, although some of us were quite poor from fatigue and exposure."[12]

Upon returning to Kirtland, the deceased soldier's family was notified in person as to the death of their loved one. Surplus clothing and other personal items returned. It was said that their son, brother, husband was buried in graves on a hill near the bank of Rush Creek, Missouri.

Some have the misconception that cholera only hit upon Zion's Camp. This is totally untrue. Many were burning their dead. By midsummer 1834 cholera was rapidly decimating the population of Missouri. In St. Louis alone seven thousand people perished in five weeks. But with its customary indiscrimination the plague struck down the godly as well as the godless.[13]

Joseph Smith stated, "The moment I attempted to rebuke the disease I was attacked, and had I not desisted in my attempt to save the life of a brother, I would have sacrificed my own."[14]

This chapter was a dark day for the Lord's Army and we close it as the Day the Bodies Burned on Rush Hill and do honor to their names.

Fallen Soldiers	Death
Eben Wilcox	25 June 1834
John S. Carter	25 June 1834
Seth Hitchcock	25 June 1834
Erastus Rudd	25 June 1834
Alfred Fisk	26 June 1834
Edward Ives	26 June 1834
Noah Johnson	26 June 1834
Jesse B. Lawson	26 June 1834
Robert McCord	26 June 1834
Elial Strong	26 June 1834
Warren Ingalls	26 June 1834
Sidney Gilbert	29 June 1834
Jesse J. Smith	1 July 1834
[Parkin]	[No date]

{Newsletter #14, Jackson County, Missouri Summer 1997 – Title: Zion's Camp Monument}[15]

On 14 February 1835, Joseph Smith visiting with Brigham Young and Joseph Young at his house, made the following statement, "Brethren, I have seen those men who died of the cholera in our camp; and the Lord knows, if I get a mansion as bright as theirs, I ask no more." At this he wept and could not speak for some time.[16]

NOTES:

1. Journal of Joseph Bates Noble, Typescript, BYU-S, p. 3.

2. Newsletter #14 Jackson County, Missouri Summer 1997 – Zion's Camp Monument, p. 1.

3. Journal of Joseph Bates Noble, Typescript, BYU-S, p. 3.

4. Ibid, p. 3.

5. Ibid, p. 3.

6. Columbia University Medical Guide, 1985, p. 522.

7. C.C. Rich Journal, cited p. 167.   Also Jackson County Newsletter #14, Missouri, Summer 1997.

8. Journal of Joseph Bates Noble, Transcript BYU-S, p. 4.

9. Ibid, p. 4.

10. Newsletter #14, Jackson County, Missouri, Summer 1997, Title: Zion's Camp Monument, p. 2 (Martin Diary).

11. Journal of Joseph Bates Noble, Transcript BYU-S, p. 4.

12. Ibid, p. 4.

13. No Man Knows My History, by Fawn M. Brodie, 2nd Edition, 1986, p. 157.

14. Ibid., p. 157

15. Newsletter #14, Jackson County, Missouri, Summer 1997, Title: Zion's Camp Monument.

16. Essentials in Church History by Joseph Fielding Smith, 1960, pp. 180-181.

THE LOST SEVENTY 5

Bates Noble, "After spending the next four months on foot and man wagon traveling 2,000 miles round trip then returned to Kirtland in late August tired and somewhat broke; I stayed in Kirtland one week to rest, and have my clothes washed. I had agreed with Joseph Coe to tend his mill for $300 per year. A house and lot and fire wood sweeping of mill. I then borrowed money from a friend with a hand shake, sealed the loan, used part to buy a wedding ring, placed an undetermined amount of cash within a bundle of unused surplus clothing and attached a note in care of Eben Wilcox." [1]

The balance of the cash was pocket change for Bates in making his way two hundred miles towards his father's family. Why the money in care of Eben Wilcox? Like an older brother, Eben taught Bates the mill trade; also they were baptized on the same day. Bates was his best man at his wedding. The two soldiers traveled the dusty trail covering one thousand miles to Zion's Camp, cholera struck suddenly, and Eben died in the care of his friend. The bundle of money was sent to Catherine Noramore Wilcox and little six year-old daughter Adelia Almira Wilcox. Bates heart was very heavy at this time and he longed to get home.

He continues, "I then went to Fairport (fifteen miles), got aboard a steamboat, and in twenty-four hours landed in Buffalo, good passage (two hundred miles) by stage. I went to my father's [a] distance of forty miles. I found them all well; my mother's joy was full at the sight of her dear boy (as she often called me). "Oh," she says, "What have you accomplished? You have come very near losing your life. How poor you are. How you have tanned up." Every kindness that I could expect from parents were shown me. They, with my brothers and sisters, welcomed me home."

"I stayed with them three or four days, and then went to see the person that had won my affections—may I not say, had possession of my heart more than two years before I left for Missouri. I formed an acquaintance with Mary A. Beman. I found Mr. Beman and family all well. They all welcomed my return, especially my dear Mary, whose heart, like the fawn, leaped for joy. She was still engaged in teaching in a large district school. I told her what my calculations were; as soon as I could I wished to return to Kirtland, Ohio."[2]

"She was willing to have her lot cast with mine, although at this time was not a Mormon (or had not been baptized). I made my wishes known to her parents. They gave their consent and the time was set for our marriage. The whole family connection was invited to attend. We were married Thursday p.m., at 5, September 11, 1834. The more part of our relatives were present. The large commodious room was filled to overflowing. We had an excellent supper and pleasant interview with our friends. However, the thought of our leaving their society and moving off for Ohio was sorrowful, for as yet the family were so closely settled down together that in one-half days' drive they could all come together. So it had been for a number of years. They were in the practice of coming together twice a year for a feast. But now the scene is about to be changed. The youngest but two about to break the tie. They made liberal offers to me if I would settle down among them, but no, my eyes had seen the light that shone forth in the West and I felt determined to follow it. I prepared myself with a horse and wagon, and one week after our marriage we started for the Ohio. Her parents had given her a good fit-out from everything we could take and money to buy the rest."[3]

Bates and his new bride traveled six days by horse and wagon. Their wagon was full with house giving gifts and money in their pockets. Bates, "I must say one of the most pleasant times I ever before witnessed."[4]

The two traveled the two hundred miles arriving in Kirtland on the 24th day of September. They unloaded the house goods into their log house. "I found things prepared for me as we had agreed on. We then went to Richmond, and I got such things we needed for keeping house and went immediately to keeping house, having things very comfortable."[5]

October, November, December and January passed our newlyweds in the blinking of an eye and Bates received a special invite by the Prophet. "On Saturday the 14th of February, 1835, a two day conference was convened, at which, after a weeks notice, those brethren who had accompanied the Prophet to Missouri in the camp were called together, and it was announced that from their numbers would be chosen the Quorum of the Twelve Apostles and their assistants in the church, The Seventy."[6]

Bates Noble also attended the next conference on the 28th of February. To his surprise he was called to be a General Authority in the First Quorum of the Seventy. Some say that he was third on the list.

Bates said, "About this time the Lord manifested to President Joseph Smith that it was necessary to select (or call) twelve men to be apostles (or special witnesses) to form a quorum equal in authority to that of the First Presidency. It was then said to Joseph Smith, "Call a Seventy, and ordain them out of Zion's hand." The names of the Twelve were, Thomas B. Marsh, Brigham Young, Heber C. Kimball,

Orson Hyde, P. P. Pratt, Orson Pratt, Lyman Johnson, Luke Johnson, William McClellan, William Smith, Jerod Patton, and John Boynton. *I was one of the Seventies. I was appointed a mission in the spring after this ordination.*"[7]

B.H. Roberts stated that the Quorum of the Twelve are declared to be "equal in authority and power" to the Presidency of the Church; and the First Quorum of the Seventy form a quorum "equal in authority to the Quorum of the Twelve Apostles".[8]

Joseph Fielding Smith said, "The meeting was called and selection was made from those who went to Missouri in Zion's Camp to create the First Quorum of Seventy. Hagen Aldrich, Joseph Young, Levi W. Hancock, Leonard Rich, Zebedee Coltren, Lyman Sherman and Sylvester Smith were called to the office of Presidents of this Quorum of Seventy. These brethren and those appointed to form the Quorum were ordained under the hands of the First Presidency".[9]

Directly following this special conference Joseph Bates Noble was set apart under the hands of the First Presidency of the Church of Jesus Christ of Latter Day Saints. He was now a member of the First Quorum of Seventy.

The Prophet Joseph Smith emphasized the qualifications for the new priesthood callings: "Brethren, some of you are angry with me, because you did not fight in Missouri; but let me tell you, God did not want you to fight. He could not organize His kingdom with twelve men to open the gospel door to the nations of the earth, and with seventy men under their direction to follow in their tracks, unless he took them from a body of men who had offered their lives, and who had made as great a sacrifice as did Abraham. Now the Lord has got his Twelve and His Seventy, and there will be other quorums of seventy called, who will make the sacrifice, and those who have not made their sacrifices and their offerings now, will make them here after."[10]

Researching the Improvement Era, April 1935, I came across an article titled 'THE SEVENTY' by Antoine R. Ivins, a member of the First Council of the Seventy. It should be noted that it was edited by Joseph Fielding Smith.

Joseph Fielding Smith said, "Like many others of our institutions, the Seventy had its inception in the time when records keeping was an undeveloped art and the detailed information as to its organization is in many instances lost. We are wont to say that the First Quorum of the Seventy of our dispensation was organized by the Prophet Joseph Smith on the 28th day of February, 1835, just a century ago. On this day forty-five men were selected, "blessed and ordained" to form the nucleus of the First Quorum".[11]

The 1935 Improvement Era shows forty-five men listed as set apart in the First Quorum of Seventy, twenty-four face pictures accompany twenty-four names, pictures are missing on some men, and sadly six blanks without names. Pictures go from pages 213-215. Joseph Bates Noble is one of the missing names. Here is the list, with the name of Joseph Bates Noble added to it.

Latter Day First Quorum of the Seventy

1.	Hazen Aldrich	2.	Joseph Young
3.	Levi W. Hancock	4.	Zebedee Coltren
5.	Leonard Rich	6.	Lyman Sherman
7.	Sylvester Smith	8.	John Gould
9.	James Foster	10.	Daniel S. Miles
11.	Josiah Butterfield	12.	Salmon Gee
13.	John Gaylord	14.	Henry Harriman
15.	Zera Pulsipher	16.	Albert P. Rockwell
17.	Benjamin L. Clapp	18.	Jedediah M. Grant

19.	Horace S. Eldrege	20.	Jacob Gates
21.	John Vancott	22.	William W. Taylor
23.	Abraham H. Cannon	24.	Seymour B. Young
25.	C. D. Fjeldsted	26.	John Morgan
27.	Brigham H. Roberts	28.	George Reynolds
29.	Edward Stevenson	30.	Joseph W. McMurrin
31.	Charles H. Hart	32.	Rey L. Pratt
33.	Jonathan Golden Kimball	34.	Rulon S. Wells
35.	Levi Ergar Young	36.	Antoine R. Ivins
37.	Samuel Otis Bennion	38.	John H. Taylor
39.	Rufus K. Hardy	40.	***Joseph Bates Noble***
41.	{Blank}	42.	{Blank}
43.	{Blank}	44.	{Blank}
45.	{Blank}[12]		

Hopefully, someday in the future the numbers 41-42-43-44-45 will fall into place with a name and picture. Family research is the key to follow in giving due honor to the missing names.

NOTES:

1. Journal of Joseph Bates Noble, Typescript BYU-S, pp. 4-5.

2. Ibid, pp. 4-5.

3. Ibid, pp. 4-5.

4. Ibid, p. 5.

5. Ibid, p. 5.

6. Ibid, p. 5.

7. Ibid, p. 5.

8. Comprehensive History of the Church, Vol. I, by B. H. Roberts, 1965, pp. 371-372.

9. Essentials in Church History, 16th Edition, by Joseph Fielding Smith, 1960, p. 182. Also, for the names of those who formed this Quorum of Seventy see the Documentary History of the Church, Vol. 2:203.

10. Comprehensive History of the Church, Vol. I, 1965, pp. 377-378.

11. The Improvement Era, Joseph Fielding Smith, April 1935, p. 213.

12. Ibid, p. 213.

"ARISE BROTHER NOBLE"

The Prophet stood on a river bank point so high in the mid of day that he could see from its summit a great river cutting a silver semicircle at his feet. The spot was wooded, trackless, and with beautiful swamp land covering the low lands behind him. "It is a beautiful site", he said fervently, "and it shall be called Nauvoo, which means in Hebrew a beautiful plantation"[1].

Bates Noble commented, "We soon commenced to move our families up the river about fifty miles, to a place called Commerce, afterwards Nauvoo. Quite a number of us crossed the Mississippi River, to the Iowa side, to avail ourselves of some log cabins that had formerly been used as barracks for soldiers, at a place called Montrose."

"Many saints were weakened by hunger and exposure. They fell easy victims to typhoid, malaria, and some died like flies in the first frost. Joseph and Emma Smith gave up their log house to the sick and spent the winter in a tent. Emma was considered an herb doctor and went among the sick administering Sappington's pills, Dover's powder, and various medications. Cries for blessings were so insistent that most of the days were spent making the rounds visiting the sick."

"I and some of my family were attacked with bilious fever. I think I can safely say that one half of the families of the whole people had more or less sickness, and many died. Two of my children were buried and I was nigh unto death. So low was I that my wife asked me, in tears, if I was dying".[2]

Meanwhile on the opposite side of the river in Commerce Joseph Smith and family had filled their house with the sick. Emma and Joseph were constantly attending to their wants, nevertheless the Prophet soon felt sick himself. After being confined to his bed for several days, on the morning of July 22, 1839, Joseph suddenly arose from his bed and commenced to administering to the sick in his own house.

"The Prophet commanded them in the name of the Lord Jesus Christ to arise and be made whole; and the sick were healed upon every side of him".[3]

After healing all that lay sick upon the bank of the river, he called upon Elder Kimball and some others to accompany him across the river to visit the sick. He visited Brigham Young and family, Wilford Woodruff, Orson Pratt, John Taylor, and in the name of Jesus Christ they also arose and accompanied him.

The company next visited Joseph Bates Noble, who lay very sick. He was also healed by the Prophet. Bates states, "At this time Brother Elijah Fordham, a next-door neighbor to me, was very sick; indeed they were preparing clothes for his burial. In this trying hour the Holy Ghost was poured out upon the Prophet Joseph Smith, and he, with Brothers Brigham Young, Heber C. Kimball, Parley P. Pratt and others, came to Brother Fordham's house and commanded him, in the name of Jesus Christ, to arise and walk. He immediately jumped from his dying bed, kicked off the drafts from his feet, and came into my house, following the brethren, and shouting, leaping, and praising God with all his might."

"President Smith, while leading the way to my bed, made this remark: "Brother Noble, you have been too long with me to lie here." As soon as I saw him the tears of joy burst from my eyes. In a moment he was by my bedside and took me by the hand. Without waiting for the other brethren to get to my bed, he commanded me, in the name of Jesus Christ to arise and walk. I arose, and while putting on my clothes I fainted. When I regained consciousness I was on the bed, and Joseph was standing close to me. As soon as my eyes met his he said, "Wherefore didst thou doubt?" and again commanded me to arise".

"While he was speaking I felt the healing virtue flowing through every part of my system. I immediately arose and walked rejoicing and praising the Lord with all my heart, for His blessing resting upon me, by which I was made whole".[4]

During this time the wicked became alarmed and followed the company into Brother Noble's house. After Brother Noble was healed, all kneeled down to pray. Brother Fordham was mouth, and while praying, he fell to the floor. The Prophet arose, and on looking around he saw quite a number of unbelievers in the house, whom he ordered out. When the room was cleared of the wicked, Brother Fordham came to the floor and finished the prayer.[5]

"Brother Fordham was more active and stronger than I was. He never sat down in my house, but as soon as Brother Joseph had given directions to my wife concerning some nourishment for me, he left with the rest of the brethren. They went and administered to others who were sick, and called them up in a similar manner".[6]

After the healing of Brother Noble and the sick in Montrose, all the company followed Joseph to the bank of the river, where he was going to take the boat to return home. While waiting for the boat a man from the west, who had seen that the sick and dying were healed, asked Joseph if he would not go to his house and heal two of his children who were very sick. They were twins and were three months old.

Joseph told the man he could not go, but he would send someone to heal them. He told Elder Woodruff to go with the man and heal his children. At the same time he took from his pocket a silk bandana handkerchief and gave it to Brother Woodruff, telling him to wipe the faces of the children with it, and they shall be healed; and remarked at the same time, "As long as you keep that handkerchief it shall remain a league between you and me." Elder Woodruff did as he was commanded, and the children were healed.[7]

Stepping forward into Bates' life, he reflected many times upon this healing day. Nearing age ninety, he could still feel the virtue of the Latter Day Prophet on that special day. The voice of the Lord speaking through His Prophet commanding, "Arise Brother Noble, you have been to long with me to lie here".[8]

NOTES:

1. No Man Knows My History, by Fawn M. Brodie, 2nd Edition, 1962, p. 256.

2. Journal of Joseph Bates Noble – Autobiography Typescript, BYU-S, p. 6.

3. Testimony given by Wilford Woodruff in his journal and noted as such in "A Comprehensive History of the Church" Vol. II, by B. H. Roberts, 1965, pp 21-22.

4. Journal of Joseph Bates Noble – Autobiography Typescript, BYU-S, p. 6. Also A Comprehensive History of the Church by B. H. Roberts, Vol. II, 1965, p. 22. (The company next visited Brother Joseph Bates Noble, who lay very sick, and so on...).

5. Leaves from My Journal, Wilford Woodruff, ch xix. Also History of the Church, Period I, Vol. IV, pp. 3-5. This incident is also detailed at some length in Parley P. Pratt's Autobiography, p. 325.

6. Journal of Joseph Bates Noble – Autobiography Typescript, BYU-S, p. 6.

7. Leaves from My Journal, Wilford Woodruff, ch xix. Also History of the Church by B.H. Roberts, 1962, p. 22.

8. Journal of Joseph Bates Noble – Autobiography Typescript, BYU-S, p. 6.

MAJOR NOBLE —
NAUVOO LEGION

Gordon Bennett, the Urban Editor of the New York Herald on January 19, 1842 published the following editorial:

"Here is a new prophet, starting into existence in the green valleys and lovely little hills of the town of Manchester, in Ontario County, New York – leaving New York as Moses left Egypt – wandering over the wild prairies of the west as the great Jewish law giver wandered over the wilderness of Zion – and ultimately establishing a holy city and a new religious empire on the Mississippi, that numbers 10,000 persons in the city and 30,000 beyond its limits with a splendid temple for public worship and a military organization of 1,500 "pretty well" disciplined troops".[1]

The new city of Nauvoo saw a spectacular growth and it was laid out in neat squares like checkerboards shaped to fit a hill. The square on the summit was set aside for the beautiful temple. After one year it boasted two hundred and fifty houses along with scores more being built. Timber from the swamps had been cut and drained, neatly fenced farms fanned out from the city center leaving a memory of some wood and marsh land.

The people were friendly and hospitable to the hundreds of tourists who would soon arrive to visit the beautiful city. Steamboats were plying up and down the river and stopped regularly to discharge visitors. These visits were mostly conducted on a city tour. The city tour included a view of the summit to where the temple of the Lord was now under construction or close to completion.

The tour also included the brick houses lining the street including the Nobles'. Bates being a very industrious man built a beautiful brick house on Main Street in Nauvoo. He also acquired a large farm south of Montrose. He raised cattle, planted fruit trees and grew some produce.

Spring 1841, is the year he built the three story house. He enclosed a full basement with native limestone. The reddish bricks were burned locally and the wood portions of the structure came from the pineries of Wisconsin. He also dug a well and lined it with stone. Bates built other buildings including a carriage house, and out-buildings customary for this time period. He also laid a brick walkway to the well and outbuildings.[2]

Mary A. Beman the sweetheart of his life kept the house in good order and at times fueled the fire into the two fireplaces, one on the main floor and the other upstairs for the bedrooms. Excellent cook, homemaker and totally devoted to her husband and family.

To protect the city from future harm, if any, the Prophet organized the Nauvoo Legion. It was looked upon as the Army of the Lord. The men drilled regularly and strenuously and boasted smartly uniformed officers. The able body men between ages eighteen and forty-five were compelled to join. By January ending of 1842, the Legion ranks consisted of one thousand five hundred men approximately.[3]

Joseph requested and received from Governor Carlin of Illinois the commission of Lieutenant General over the newly organized Nauvoo Legion. His uniform was smartly designed and a blue coat with a plentiful supply of gold braid, buff trousers, high military boots, and handsome chapeau topped with ostrich feathers and on his hip he carried the Legion Sword, and two big horse-pistols. On holiday celebrations and parades he called out the Legion and led the marching riding upon his magnificent black stallion called Charlie. Bates was also on hand during these events, ranked as a major and rode along side the Prophet.[4]

Major Noble as a commissioned officer was required to take an oath of office, similar to the oath mandated in the United States Army. Regardless of rank or assignment the oath followed the same wording and form for each office.

Joseph Bates Noble, "I do solemnly swear that I will support the Constitution of the United States, and this State, and that I will not be engaged in dueling, either directly or indirectly, during my continuance in office; and that I will faithfully discharge the duties of <u>Major</u>, in the <u>Regiment</u> of the Nauvoo Legion of Illinois militia, to the best of my skill and understanding so help me God."[5]

He was required to wear a uniform. Exactly what parts of the uniform was constructed by a tailor or the soldier is unknown. Nevertheless, it is clear that Bates' uniform and other officers were patterned after in most respects identical to the United States Army uniform.

He wore a military style jacket made from navy blue wool with black cotton lining. His uniform sported nine brass buttons marked "Life Guard N.L." indicating he was also used as a bodyguard to Lt. General Joseph Smith. This clothing was accompanied by a black belt, a red or wine-colored sash that often had tassels attached to either

THE PROPHET JOSEPH ADDRESSING THE NAUVOO LEGION.

Unsheathing his sword the Prophet said: "I call God and angels to witness that this people shall have their legal rights or my blood shall be spilt upon the ground and my body consigned to the tomb but if there is one drop of blood shed on this occasion, the sword shall never again be sheathed until Christ comes to reign on earth."

end. High military boots that reached the bottom of the knee were frequently worn by higher ranking officers, while a military boot to mid-calf was for the lower ranking officers, and a black laced boot was worn by enlisted men.[6]

Bates was now the commanding officer for a battalion which consisted of a minimum of fifty-four men; to a maximum of two hundred and six. As an officer he, being a major, was above a captain and below a lieutenant colonel.[7]

Major Noble and Captain Rockwell each carried a captains' sword. Both men stood nearly the same height. The two swords measured thirty-three inches in length being designed for a man somewhat short in stature. Lt. General Joseph Smith's sword from tip to end measures forty-one inches and designed for a tall man. Captain Rockwell's sword has a sheath and hilt (handle) made of brass with a leather wrapped handle and a single hand protector following the outline of a standard light bulb in shape.[8]

Brigham Young gives an interesting physical description of Porter Rockwell. "The door of the hall was flung open and a barbaric figure, hard ridden through miles of flying dust and unwashed haste, flung himself into the room. The old slouch hat was drawn upon a mass of braided hair wound round and round the bullet-shaped face. The hooked nose, the sleepy-lidded eyes half-closed upon the eagle glance of the Mormon Scout, Indian fighter."[9]

Bates being the man he was never missed any military maneuvers. Often visitors in Nauvoo would line up on the main street just down from the temple under construction to watch the Nauvoo Legion maneuver and parade to martial music. What they witnessed was a well-drilled infantry in squads showing their new equipment – cannons, rifles, sabers (swords with a curved blade), uniforms, and a serious glint in their eyes.[10]

He with his fellow officers rode in full uniform upon fine-looking mounts saddled with the latest and best, with Joseph and Hyrum at their head. These Legion officers with every military rank in order moved down the main thoroughfare of Nauvoo in a never-to-be-forgotten sight.

On one such occasion, the military spirit infected all the boys in Nauvoo. The boys paraded and drilled with as much zest as their fathers. Josephs' eldest son, who was a member of the boys' army, took part on the memorable occasion when they decided to invade Nauvoo. The Legion, prepared to give the boys a good scare, line up to meet them. The men didn't know that the boys had raided their mothers' kitchens for every available pot and pan in the city. The boys charged out of the woods, beating on the kettles and shrieking. The Legion Army horses went into panic and refused to charge. The Prophet watching the scene mounted on the imperturbable Charlie spurred the big stallion forward into the oncoming boys. The boys scattered nimbly and the invasion of Nauvoo was repelled and Joseph Smith became the hero of the day. It was a day of fun for the sons and fathers with treats afterwards to celebrate the occasion.[11]

There were other tall officers in the Legion; however not as stocky, sturdy and thickly built as the Prophet. Hyrum's profile was somewhat thinner and sharper with a full head of brown hair and was somewhat darker than the prophet.

Hyrum being commissioned as a Major General is one step lower than a Lieutenant General. His rank allowed him to ride along side Lt. General Joseph Smith. He also stood out in full officers' uniform and one could not help but notice the likeness between the two brothers.[12] The other three Smith brothers also played an important part within the Nauvoo Legion. Don Carlos was ranked as a Brigadier General, William ranked as a Major and Samuel was ranked as a bodyguard.[13]

The year 1841 witnessed one of the most memorable parades ever displayed by the Legion. April 6 was the day of a general parade; it was the first parade held of this type in the early history of the Church. Noted as the day the cornerstones of the Nauvoo Temple were to be laid. It also marked the eleventh anniversary of the Church.[14]

On this special historical day, the Nauvoo Legion, fifteen hundred strong, arrived at the temple site. Lt. General Smith, Maj. General Hyrum Smith, Brig. General Don Carlos Smith, Maj. William Smith, and Samuel H. Smith as an officer bodyguard; and bodyguard Maj. Bates Noble with Capt. Rockwell were the first. The generals and their staff created the inner formation of a square, and the infantry and cavalry formed the outer formation with the ladies, gentlemen, children and visitors sandwiched in between the Legion force. The number was in the thousands. Lt. General Joseph Smith addressed the assembled Legion, people, visitors, and praised the Legion for their services and accomplishments of that particular day.[15]

Four months later a great loss came upon the Nauvoo Legion and the Smith family. August 7, 1841, Brig. General Don Carlos Smith died at age twenty-five. He was elected to the high office at only twenty-four years of age. Don was also commissioned to the office of Major in the Hancock Militia and later to a Lt. Col.[16]

Looking at history and enrollment; the U.S. Army was listed in 1844 at 8,453 men. 1844, was the year the Nauvoo Legion reached its highest enrollment with three thousand militia men. Looking at midway as a comparison, 1842 has been recorded at two thousand men.[17]

The Nauvoo Legion was unique by attaching the title "Legion" to its troops. Up until 1840, only once before in U.S. history did any unit attempt to use the same title. This took place in 1792 when the President of the United States reorganized the U.S. Army into a body called the Legion of the United States.[18]

What about the weapons in the Nauvoo Legion; were they Illinois State armed or privately owned? Weapons just as parade horses were apart of the proper military uniforms. Some soldiers sported two flint lock pistols, a sword fitted to one's height and rank; and a musket rifle. Some swords were nearly four feet long with elaborately ornamental hilts attached to a large black belt.[19]

The total state weapons possessed included three cannons and two hundred fifty small arms. The swords and other weapons were purchased by the militia men or funded by the Nauvoo Legion. The only exception was Lt. General Joseph Smith's sword; it was acquired by the Prophet in the early 1830's. He carried the sword during Zion's Camp march.[20]

The existence of the Nauvoo Legion as a formidable fighting force ended on Monday June 24, 1844. It was on this day that the state arms were confiscated from the storehouse.[21] It was the day Joseph, Hyrum and party headed towards Carthage.

ROSTER ABBREVIATIONS

Lieutenant General	Lt. General
Major General	Maj. General
Colonel	Col.
Major	Maj.
Brigadier General	Brig. General
Sergeant	Serg.
Quarter Master	Q-M
Paymaster	P-M
Inspector	Inspt.
Adjutant	Adj.
Aide-De-Camp	A-D-C
Captain	Capt.
Assistant	Asst.
Brevet	Brev.
Drill Officer	D-O
Chaplain	Chap.
Cavalry	Cav.
Corporal	Corp.
Herald & Armor Bearer	H-A-B
Judge Advocate	Jud. Ad. [22]

NOTES:

1. New York Herald, Gordon Bennett, Urban Editor, January 19, 1842, article.

2. Noble – Smith House, a publication of Nauvoo Restoration, Inc., P.O. Box 215, Nauvoo, Illinois, 62354. (Note: Joseph Bates Noble deeded his house to Lucy Mack Smith upon leaving Nauvoo, February 1846.)

3. Lee County Democrat, Vol. 1, No. 43, p. 2, follows: "Nauvoo Legion parade in Nauvoo, about 1500 troops – 3000 ladies and gentlemen from surrounding country attended".

4. Daughters of the Utah Pioneers Memorial Museum, 300 North Main, Salt Lake City, Utah. Display Uniforms – Basement (1) Military Room. Bodyguard uniform. Also, Revised Statutes of the State of Illinois, (Springfield, 1845), p. 302.

5. A History of the Nauvoo Legion in Illinois, Dept. of Church History, BYU, by John Sweeney, Jr., April 1974, p. 75.

6. Daughters of the Utah Pioneers Memorial Museum, 300 North Main, Salt Lake City, Utah. Display Uniforms – Basement (1) Military Room. Bodyguard uniform. Also, Lamar Noble, great grandson to Joseph Bates Noble and "Keeper of the Sword" related this information in November 2007.

7. A History of the Nauvoo Legion in Illinois, Dept. of Church History, BYU, by John Sweeney, Jr., April 1974, p. 30.

8. Sword, Scabbard displayed at the LDS Church Museum, Salt Lake City, Utah, under Joseph Smith's display window, sword belongs to Capt. O. P. Rockwell.

9. The Life Story of Brigham Young, by Gates and Widtsoe, 1st edition, 1930, p. 191.

10. Hyrum Smith, by Pearson H. Corbett, 1963, p. 315.

11. Saints Herald, January 1, 1935. Juanita Brooks, John Doyle Lee; Zealot, Pioneer, Builder, Scapegoat (Glendale, California: Arthur H. Clark Company, 1962), pp. 69-70.

12. A History of the Nauvoo Legion in Illinois, Dept. of Church History at BYU, by John Sweeney, Jr., April 1974, pp. 205-206.

13. Ibid, p. 206.

14. Legion Minutes, p. 9.

15. Ibid, p. 9.

16. History of the Church, Vol. 4, p. 400. by B. H. Roberts. Also, Times and Seasons, August 16, 1846.

17. The History of the United States Army, (New York and London, 1942), pp. 99-103.

18. Reference: Minutes and Ordinance of Organization of the Nauvoo Legion, February 3, 1841 to October 20, 1844, located in the Church of Jesus Christ of Latter Day Saints Historical Department, p. 6-7.

19. Revised Statues of the State of Illinois (Springfield, 1845), p. 302.

20. Thomas Ford, A History of Illinois, (Chicago: A.C. Griffs and Company, 1854), pp. 184-185.

21. History of the Church, by B. H. Roberts, Vol. 6, pp. 555-558.

22. A History of the Nauvoo Legion in Illinois, by John Sweeny Jr., April 1974, BYU Dept. of church History, p. 182. (Roster Abbreviations for military ranks.)

THE
AMERICAN SWORD

8

Before 1840 American swords were imported from Europe and were considered the best type blade for officer swords. The hilt handles were manufactured domestically by silver smith tradesmen. Any other type of sword blade was referred to as substandard and for this reason the U.S. Government made a decision to reform all military swords.[1]

Ames Manufacturing Company received the 1840 U.S. Army contract. This company started out manufacturing swords as early as 1830 producing the model M1832. More than likely Lt. General Joseph Smith's sword was a model M1832 custom made sword. This is just an opinion on my part as the Legion Sword is unmarked or the model number is hidden away with age.[2]

Any cavalry saber sword before 1839 and purchased from Ames Company was usually considered a badge of rank and status for the officer.[3] Joseph Smith's sword is a cavalry saber and looked upon as a badge of rank. It was designed for a high ranking officer or commander. On the other hand Maj. Noble and Capt. Rockwell's swords were different with a hilt handle designed for a regular officer.[4]

One point of interest, Ames Manufacturing Company produced more military type swords for the U.S. Army than any other company before or since. There was an estimated 200,000 swords in service by the end of the Civil War.[5]

They also made a Model M1840 cavalry sword uniquely borrowed from the French Theorists and considered an officer's sword. Any cavalry saber sword before 1839 and purchased from Ames Manufacturing Co. was usually privately ordered.[6]

Other ranking swords carried by infantry included a non-commissioned officer sword, foot artillery sword, musicians' sword, and a light artillery saber. The non-commissioned officer's sword and light artillery saber saw very little practical use and were mostly ornamental.[7]

Joseph Smith's sword was looked upon as a model sword for other officers. Regarding swords the Book of Mormon makes an interesting comment. Nephi states, "And I, Nephi, did take the sword of Laban, and after the manner of it did make many swords, lest by any means the people who were now called Lamanites should come upon us."[8]

Looking for swords at the Daughters of the Utah Pioneer Memorial Museum, I found a military section with a window display of eleven officer swords. The swords unsheathed are crisscrossed under glass and wired in the center forming a wheel. The swords vary in blade length and are manufactured by Ames Manufacturing Company.[9] Referring to the sword plate picture from the 1861 U.S. Ordnance Manual; the eleven sword display match as a cavalry saber sword with brass hilts and a leather handle.[10]

The Prophet's sword is somewhat different being older and sometimes referred to as a wrist breaker as to the design of the hilt. The hilt is not of brass and differs in that an ear extends from the hilt reflecting a French pattern design. The eleven swords at the Museum lack this ear and the hilt is made of brass.

In 2007 Lamar Noble, keeper of Joseph Smith's legion sword, noticed a small rust spot next to the base of the hilt and attempted to clean the little spot. He made a wise decision by stopping. A close inspection shows a luster of silver in color on the hilt. Personally I like the antique look as it appears old and precious in surviving from a distant past.[11]

Ames Manufacturing Company M1840 officer swords were manufactured from 1840-1860. The M1860 model swords are a look a like to the model 1840 and the only difference being the M1860 is lighter in weight.

As noted above there are eleven swords on display at the DUP Memorial Museum. Let's look at information on five of the eleven swords[12]:

Accession # 4962-002 is a sword noted as manufactured by Ames Mfg. Co. Cabotville 1851 on the blade. The sword belonged to William P. Pall a Major in the Utah Militia.[13]

Accession # 802-002 is a sword used by Henry Grow, pioneer of 1851 while marching and playing in the band, member of the Nauvoo Legion.[14]

Sword # 9723 belonged to Edward Morgan and used in the Black Hawk War. Donor is Douglas Morgan. Trademark – Ames Mfg. Co. / Serial # V8865. Materials: metal – steel – brass – leather. Color: silver – black – gold.[15]

Sword # 6776 belonged to George Davis, pioneer of 1859 with little information. W1"x41"L.[16]

One other sword owned by Colonel Reddick Newton of the Nauvoo Legion, pioneer of 1849. Donor is Madge Allred Christenson.[17]

Several swords were used in the Black Hawk War. It started on 9 April 1865. The war lasted three years with seventy-five Indians killed and five wounded. As many as twenty-five hundred soldiers were involved in the suppression of the Indian hostilities. Shortly after the war a religious awakening was among the Black Hawk Indians with several thousand entering the waters of baptism.[18]

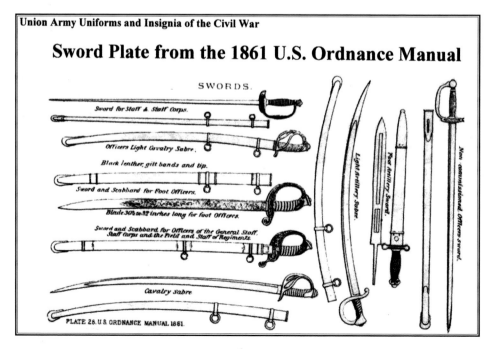

Union Army Uniforms and Insignia of the Civil War

Sword Plate from the 1861 U.S. Ordnance Manual

In retrospect just a few swords are somewhat similar to the Prophet Joseph Smith's legion sword.

Reference: Sword plate picture – 1861 U.S. Ordnance Manual. The eleven swords match with the cavalry saber sword. The swords have brass hilts and a leather handle. The Model 1840 is an Ames Company sword.

NOTES:

1. Mfg. of Regulation Model Enlisted Swords – during the Civil War, by Mike McWatters. (http://www.angelfire.com/wa/swordcollector/marks/page1htm)

2. Ames Mfg. Sword Co., 1829-1935, by John Hamilton, 1983. (http://www.amesmanufacturingco.com)

3. Ibid.

4. The author making a comparison between Lt. General Joseph Smith's sword as to Captain Porter Rockwell's legion sword (picture comparison).

5. Ames Manufacturing Sword Co., 1829-1935, by John Hamilton, 1983. http://www.amesmanufacturingco.com.

6. Ibid.

7. http://www.amesmanufacturingco.com or refer to: The 1861 U.S. Sword Ordnance Manual (http://howardlanham.tripod.com/link11d.htm).

8. Book of Mormon, 2 Nephi Chapter 5 Verse 14 regarding swords.

9. Daughters of the Utah Pioneer (DUP) Memorial Museum, 300 North Main Street, Salt Lake City, Utah. Location: Basement, under military display.

10. Sword Plate from the 1861 U.S. Ordnance Manual. Refer to picture.

11. Lamar Noble – great-grandson of Joseph Bates Noble – shared this experience with the author after inspecting the sword belonging to Joseph Smith, November 2007.

12. Refer to the picture of the eleven military swords. Picture provided by the DUP Memorial Museum, March 2008, Salt Lake City, Utah. Display – Basement military section.

13. For more information contact the Daughters of the Utah Pioneers Memorial Museum, Salt Lake City, Utah or visit http://www.dupinternational.org).

14. Ibid.

15. Ibid.

16. Ibid.

17. Ibid.

18. A Comprehensive History of the Church, Century One, Vol. V, 1965, by B. H. Roberts, pp. 149-164.

WARRANT OF DEATH AND CIRCUMSTANCES

The Nauvoo years 1839-1844 were happy years for the Prophet; nevertheless they were also filled with lawsuits, arrests, and intrigues among some of his own people. Joseph found the time to write the history of the Church and also to bring the Mormon Theology to its full flowering.

Let it be said that each migration of the saints had risen out of a special set of circumstances. The move from Kirtland and from New York had been opportunistic and the flight from Kirtland was the result of apostate rather than non-Mormon persecution. The Missouri militia expulsion was due mainly because of deeply rooted slavery and Indian issues. Mormons did not believe in slavery, and also were, somewhat, preaching the restored gospel to the Indians. Neither one of these set well with the Missourians and thus mob action against the Saints.[1]

Now the old-timers of Illinois would soon reap threats of anti-Mormonism against the Saints in Nauvoo. To them the Theocracy was a malignant tyranny that was spreading as swiftly and dangerously as a Mississippi River flood which might eventually engulf the very government of the United States. Anti-Mormonism in Illinois was much more dangerous than it had been in Missouri. Their fear was not the repugnance for polygamy; it was a rock-bound American concern of despotism.[2]

Two events also added fuel to the fire by placing a price on his head and the thought of imminent death became a constant chilling presence.

Event one, on the sixth of May, 1842 Lilburn W. Boggs, ex-governor of Missouri, was said to have been shot by an assassin. And in consequence of the injury received, suspicion immediately fell upon Joseph, who was accused of having committed the crime. This was a complete falsehood as the Prophet was, on that day, at an officer's drill in Nauvoo several hundred miles to which Boggs resided and was seen by hundreds. To make this more probable they accused Joseph of sending O.P. Rockwell into Missouri with orders to shoot the ex-Governor, and from this time on they pursued the Prophet and Porter Rockwell with all diligence.[3]

Event two, June 10, 1844 a scandalous press in Nauvoo was removed and the city council took the matter into consideration, and finding that the law would allow them to do so they declared it a public nuisance and had it treated accordingly. At this the apostates left the city in a great rage swearing vengeance against Joseph and the city council. They headed to Carthage and got out writs for Joseph including all those who were in anyway concerned in the destruction of the press.[4]

Shortly after event two, Governor Ford of Illinois came into the town of Carthage in the midst of a mob asking them to stand by him in defending the law. He organized a militia among them demanding a trial warrant to be issued calling for the arrest of Joseph and Hyrum Smith. He did not recognize the Right of Habeas Corpus granted by the City Charter of Nauvoo. They were to be arrested for treason. The warrant called for appearance at Carthage, June 24, 1844.[5]

The shooting of Governor Boggs is debatable and some say that Porter Rockwell pulled the trigger. He spent nine months in prison, part of the time in irons and eventually released sometime in 1843. Mob members also placed a price on his head. For this reason only, he did not make the trip along with the Prophet to Carthage. He kept watch over Emma Smith and family.[6]

Joseph Bates Noble head bodyguard made this trip along with the Prophet and others to Carthage. This will be covered in the next chapter.

NOTES:

1. No Man Knows My History, by Fawn M. Brodie, 2nd Edition, 1985, p. 380.

2. Ibid, pp. 381-382.

3. A Comprehensive History of the Church, Century One, Vol. II, by B. H. Roberts, 1965, p. 148.

4. Hyrum Smith – Patriarch, by Pearson H. Corbett, 1963, pp. 362-367.

5. Essentials in Church History, by Joseph Fielding Smith, 16th Edition, 1960, pp. 375-382.

6. A Comprehensive History of the Church, Century One, Vol. II, by B. H. Roberts, 1965, pp. 150-152.

TIPPED HIS HAT TO THE PROPHET

Lt. General Smith makes a visit with his wife Emma around noon Monday June 24th knowing this will be their last. Maj. Noble is riding his large horse slightly to the backside of the Prophet. Other officers from the Nauvoo Legion are attending the small convoy. Hyrum Smith soon joins up along side his brother. The return trip from Carthage will be different, it will be in caskets.

The small party of men mounted on horses, legion swords attached, dressed in army uniforms, make their way past the beautiful Nauvoo Temple staring affectionately up at its high white façade. The eyes of each swept slowly down the neat square blocks with rows of brick houses. Each home is flanked by gardens and green young orchards leading down to the swelling Mississippi River. This seems to be somewhat a pleasant June day.[1]

The Prophet makes a comment to his men, "This is the loveliest place and the best people under Heaven", he then sadly states, "Little do they know the trials that await them."[2]

The small convoy stops, Joseph twice rides "Charley", his large horse, down the dirt road and up to the mansion house to bid his family a farewell. The officers notice he is solemn, thoughtful and expressing to several expectations to be murdered. These expressions seem unreal to Maj. Noble and fellow officers.

Again, the party starts out towards Carthage. Maj. Noble in passing looks upon his house with thoughts going back to the day first meeting up with the Prophet and Hyrum in pitching hay in Kirtland. Could this possibly be the last ride?

Joseph takes a second look upon his farm field, after they passed it; he turns around several times to look once more. He comments, "If some of you had such a farm and knew you would not see it anymore, you would want to take a good look at it for the last time."[3]

Reaching the edge of Nauvoo, Joseph and company met a group of young men who marched all through the night and into the day from Ramus to join up with the Nauvoo Legion. Their leather shoes are worn thin through the soles. Many feet are cut and bleeding with blisters. Joseph's young cousin John Lyman Smith runs up flinging his arms about him. The boy's feet are bleeding and Joseph with tears in his eyes, states, "God bless you, God bless you my dear boy."

A shoemaker named Nathaniel Ashby, a close friend to Bates Noble, is standing near the door of his shop. Joseph called out, "Let these men have some shoes." "I have no shoes", shrugging stated the man. The Prophet politely yells out, "No shoes, let them have boots." These young men were fitted up with leather boots.

Lt. General Joseph Smith mounting Charlie makes a final comment to Cousin John, "These troops will be disbanded and soon returned home. I shall go to Carthage for trial with the protection of the Governor, so have no fears for you shall see Israel triumph in peace."[4]

The shoemaker's son Benjamin Ashby was working near his father's shop and makes the following observation:

"I was in my father's garden one morning, the memorable June 1844, when Joseph Smith rode past on his way to Carthage. Never shall I forget the look of deep sorrow that covered his noble countenance – that was the last time I saw him alive. He was met on the way by an officer and posse with an order from the Governor for the return of the state arms and he turned back to see the order complied with. On getting into town he called Brother J.B. Noble to accompany him and his brother Hyrum. They turned off the road, leaving the company, and to a short cut across the hills. When alone, he asked Hyrum what the spirit indicated to him. He replied that he could get no satisfactory answer. Joseph then said, "Well, if they kill me, I shall die innocent and my blood will be required of this nation, this day", near as I remember was the testimony."

Benjamin continues, "In the afternoon he went to Carthage and to his martyrdom. I sat upon the steps of my father's house on the evening of the day that he was shot until twelve o'clock and never did I hear before such an uproar and noise that seemed to pervade the very atmosphere; dogs howling, mingled with confused noises as though all the legions of the damned were in commotion."[5]

The distance from Nauvoo to Carthage is eighteen miles. It takes approximately six hours in making the trip. This time it is a one way ticket for Hyrum and Joseph. It is past noon with the sky becoming cloudy, dark, and gloomy. It is a mucky, humid day in late June. The spirits of the army convoy are somewhat down.

Occasionally, a rest stop is needed to rest the horses and company. Several hours up the dirt road a private meeting is arranged with Maj. Noble by the Prophet himself. The two horses make their way into a small ravine somewhat near the dirt roadside. Bates Noble one-on-one with his friend Joseph Smith. This was Joseph's final farewell to his trusted friend and long time bodyguard. No one knows the words that were shared at this time or the tears.

The Prophet placed into the hand of Bates two messages for delivery, one for Porter Rockwell, and the other to his sweetheart Emma. The note expressed his love to Emma. The other was to advise

Porter to stay in Nauvoo thus not delivering himself into the hands of the enemy. This would prove to be certain death for Capt. Rockwell.[6]

At this time, the Prophet stood up and presented his "Legion Sword" along with his pistol to his trusted friend as a token of their friendship. He gave a parting handclasp before each parted their way. Bates Noble was now "The Keeper of the Prophet's Sword", a trust he kept until his death bed.[7]

Bates Noble with honor carefully wrapped the "Legion Sword" of the Lt. General into the center of his bed blanket. He tucked away the pistol and placed the rolled blanket to the left side of his large horse. He placed the messages into his saddle bag, mounted onto his horse, and headed out from the small ravine. He glanced back tipping his hat to the Prophet.

Returning towards Nauvoo, he was very careful to ride up and off the dirt road to avoid any suspicion with any horseman or buggy. He was carrying two very important messages, one for Emma Smith and the other for Porter Rockwell. He could feel the parting handclasp with the Prophet into his inner spirit. This feeling carried with him throughout the remainder of his life. The big reminder was anytime he held the sword into his right hand. The sword became a comfort to him at times of depression and he could feel the spirit of a great noble one who once held this "Legion Sword" to his side. It was like repeating the parting handclasp of true friendships at the departure day.

The small army convoy continued down the road stopping off at a fellow's house just short four miles west of Carthage. The time is around 8:00 p.m. Monday. They're in wait for Capt. Dunn and greeted with refreshments much to their joy. So far it was a hard ride, dusty road, hot day, along with the stress being placed upon them.[8]

It was midnight June 24th when Joseph and Hyrum were escorted into Carthage by a well disciplined company of militia from

Carthage Jail in 1855

McDonough County. Upon arriving into the center of town, they were surrounded by the troops from Warsaw and Carthage. The militia troops met them with shouts of derision and triumph, "Stand away, you McDonough boys, and let us shoot the damn Mormons!" "God damn you, Old Joe, we've got you now!" "Clear the way and let us see Old Joe, the Prophet of God. He's seen the last of Nauvoo. We'll use him up and kill all the damned Mormons!"[9]

Joseph's mother, Lucy Mack Smith, made the following comment, "My sons were thrown into jail, where they remained three days in company with Brothers Richards, Taylor and Markham. At the end of this time, the Governor disbanded most of the men, but left a guard of eight of our bitterest enemies over the jail, and sixty more of the same character about a hundred yards distant. He then came into Nauvoo with a guard of fifty or sixty men, made a short speech, and returned immediately. During his absence from Carthage, the guards rushed Brother Markham out of the place at the point of a bayonet. Soon after this two hundred of those discharged in the morning rushed into Carthage, well armed, and painted black, red and yellow and in ten minutes fled again leaving my sons murdered and mangled corpses!"[10]

The cowardly attack was made upon the Carthage Jail, with the door kicked open shots were fired into Hyrum and the first ball striking him in the nose and stumbling backwards cried, "I am a dead man". Joseph now discharged all six barrels of the six-shooter down the hall passageway at the attackers and three balls found their mark. One replied, "Yes, my arm is all shot to pieces by Old Joe," he screamed, "but I don't care; I've got revenge; I shot Hyrum!"[11]

When Joseph looked out upon a hundred bayonets gleaming dully in the murky light, attached to every bayonet was a hideously painted face, and it must have seemed to him as if hell itself had vomited upon him and his companions. Evil was there in full force. His only escape was to jump out of the two story window. A ball from the door caught him in the backside and other balls struck him as he hit the ground. A painted man dragged him to the well-curb raising his bowie knife and rushed forward to cut off the Prophet's head. At that instant, clouds parted and the June sun blazed fully upon the scene and it seemed that a pillar of light thrust down from heaven rested between the Prophet of God and his murderers. The muskets of four that fired upon the Prophet fell to the ground and the bowie knife fell powerless from the hand of the devil. The men stood like marble statues having no power to move a single limb of their bodies. The militia men began to scatter in panic.[12]

Well at Carthage Jail in 1855.

No one in the Nauvoo Legion knew of Lt. General Joseph Smith and Maj. General Hyrum Smith's peril; surely the legion officers would have been there for a dramatic rescue. Nevertheless, even the head bodyguard Maj. Noble and Capt. Rockwell were totally unaware or would immediately been on their way. It just wasn't meant to be.

Brigham Young later in years made the following statement, "They took Joseph and Hyrum, and as a guarantee for their safety, Governor Thomas Ford pledged the faith of the State of Illinois. They were imprisoned, on the pretense of safekeeping, because the mob was so enraged and violent. The Governor left them in the hands of the mob, which entered the prison and shot them dead. After the mob had committed these murders, they came upon us and burned our houses and grain. When the brethren would go out to put the fire out, the mob would lay concealed under fences, and in the darkness of the night, they would shoot them. At last they succeeded in driving us from the state of Illinois."[13]

NOTES:

1. No Man knows My History, by Fawn M. Brodie, 2nd Edition, 1962, pp. 386-387.

2. Ibid, p. 387. Also, A Comprehensive History of the Church, Century One, Vol. II, by B. H. Roberts, 1962, p. 248.

3. Hyrum Smith, by Pearson H. Corbett, 1963, p. 394.

4. A Transcript of this manuscript account by John Lyman Smith may be seen in the Utah State Historical Society Library.

5. Benjamin Ashby Autobiography, copy of holograph, BYU-S, pp.9-10. Brother B. Noble to accompany Joseph Smith to Carthage.

6. Joseph Smith, op. cit., Vol. VI pp. 561-565. Also, Hyrum Smith by Pearson H. Corbett, 1963, p. 398. This is a message sent by Joseph Smith to O.P. Rockwell telling him not to come to Carthage, but stay in Nauvoo, and not suffer himself to be delivered in the hands of his enemies or to be taken a prisoner by anyone.

7. West Bountiful, 1848-1988, A Pictorial History by LaRue Hugoe - Edith Deppe, 1988, pp. 21-23. Also, refer to Church News - Week Ending January 15, 1966, Title: "This Week in Church History: Bishop Noble – Friend of the Prophet". By Arnold Irvine. Also refer to Journal of Joseph Bates Noble, Transcript BYU-S, p. 8.

8. Hyrum Smith, by Pearson H. Corbett, 1963, p. 395.

9. A Comprehensive History of the Church, Century One, Vol. II, by B. H. Roberts, 1965, p. 250.

10. History of Joseph Smith by Lucy Mack Smith – Mother – 1945, pp. 323-324.

11. Essentials in Church History, by Joseph Fielding Smith, 1950, pp. 382-383.

12. Autobiography of Parley P. Pratt, edited by his son, 1985, Deseret Book Company, pp. 391-392.

13. Discourses of Brigham Young, by John A. Widtsoe, 1966 Edition, p. 473.

ONE FLINTLOCK PISTOL AND TWO CAPTAIN'S SWORDS

11

The day Bishop Noble tipped his hat to the Prophet was special; he is now carrying two gifts, one is the flintlock pistol, and the other Lt. General Smith's sword. The Legion Sword is a gift to bodyguard Bates Noble and the other is a gift to bodyguard O. P. Rockwell.

Upon arriving in Nauvoo, Bates makes his way up to the Mansion House and delivers Emma her message; next he meets with Capt. Rockwell and delivers his message. Maj. Noble removes the Prophet's flintlock pistol from his saddle bag and presents the gift to Capt. Rockwell. Porter Rockwell reads his message and obeys the order given to him by his commander Lt. General Joseph Smith. Maj. Noble was also advised to stay in Nauvoo after his return.

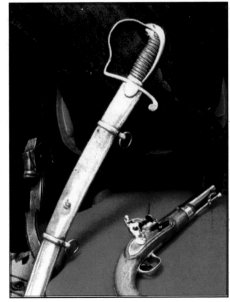

Later in life and just before his death, Porter Rockwell presented his personal captain's legion sword, a flint lock pistol and a pair of Joseph Smith's uniform epaulettes as a gift to his friend George W. Lufkin. It is speculated that the uniform epaulettes were given to

O. P. Rockwell as a special gift from Emma Smith. Emma also gave Porter Rockwell an oak casket stick from the lid of Joseph's casket; its whereabouts is not known.[1]

Joseph Smith's flintlock pistol is unique with a walnut stock and inspection stamps "NNT" and "MTL" on it. It has a brass pin and nickel hammer with USR Johnson (Midd n Conn), 1840 engraved on it. US-NWPP is engraved on the pistol barrel.[2]

The Epaulet is also impressive with its buttons and ties still in place. They came as a pair and one on the back side is bare to the metal core.[3]

Porter Rockwell's legion sword is a captains' sword. It is not the type of sword used for a Lt. General or commander. The blade measures approximately thirty three inches.[4]

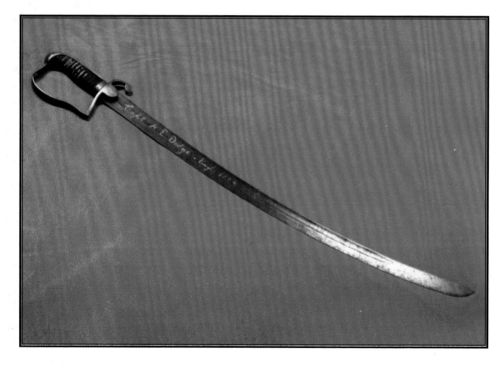

Another sword of interest is located at the Daughters of the Utah Pioneers Memorial Museum in Salt Lake City. The accession number is #1121 and cataloging date 14 Feb. 1990. The sword belonged to

Capt. A.E. Dodge and purchased in 1844 eventually making its way into the Salt Lake valley. The relic sword was used in the Black Hawk War. Stamped on the sword blade is 'Capt. A.E. Dodge'. It is written in yellow on both sides of the blade. The hilt handle is brass and wood with leather as a handle wrapped with white-twine.[5]

The interesting part regarding the captain's sword was its whereabouts; it was found close to the Jordan River by William R. Carey in April, 1933. Shortly afterward William donated the captain's sword to the Daughters of the Utah Pioneers Memorial Museum.[6]

The author highly recommends to any family or individual to visit both Museums. Each has a lot to offer and hours could be spent visiting each museum.

NOTES:

1. The Church of Jesus Christ of Latter Day Saints Museum of Church History and Art, 45 North West Temple, Salt Lake City, Utah. Joseph Smith's display window.

2. The Church of Jesus Christ of Latter Day Saints Museum of Church History and Art, 45 North West Temple, Salt Lake City, Utah. Joseph Smith's flintlock pistol is unique and on display. Donated by J.E. Cardon and originally in the possession of Capt. Rockwell.

3. Ibid.

4. Ibid.

5. Daughters of the Utah Pioneer Memorial Museum, 300 North Main, Salt Lake City, Utah. Basement (1) military room, accession # 1121, sword belonged to Capt. A.E. Dodge.

6. Ibid.

A CASKET CANE SPEAKS OUT

12

Somewhere along the bank side of the mighty Mississippi River not too far from the City of Joseph stood a huge oak tree. The axes fell upon it in the spring of 1844. It hit the ground like thunder. God's eyes were upon this particular tree for several hundred years. It was destined for a special mission.

This tree reached a height close to one hundred feet and a girth somewhere between eight to ten feet. Many old trees along the course of the river bank were close to seven times this circumference. Oak is one of our largest living trees spanning generation upon generation. Symbolically, oak is a symbol of strength, endurance, and the National Tree of the United States of America. [1]

Several oxen teams were used to ox-cart the holy tree to a lumber mill. Early in the spring of 1844 a casket maker from Nauvoo, with his lumber wagon, makes his way along a dirt road to the ship yard. Several times a year he makes this trip. His keen eyes are used in selecting only the best quality oak slabs from the center ring cut. Outward cuts from the center are knotty which could cause a break point in his caskets. A body falling onto the ground would not be good business.

The maker uses one inch thick slabs for the bottom, sides and lid. No nails, every joint is tongue and groove. Soon, two beautiful oak caskets will be crafted from the holy tree using a joint to which a tongue on the edge of one board fits into a groove on the end of another. The caskets are sanded, glued and polished to a high luster, and set aside in his shop.[2]

In quoting Glennie Kindred, "The oak is deeply connected in our hearts as representing the very essence of England, and especially the power of the High King and his ancient and spiritual link to the land. It would be hard not to think of this tree as a masculine energy – mighty, strong, enduring and steadfast."[3]

Now, let's step ahead into time, Burley Idaho, November 10, 2007 and before me on my desk is an old wooden cane made out of oak. It looks unused and carries a unique spirit. Where did it come from and how old is this cane?

It measures thirty-five inches in length and approximately one inch square from top to bottom. It has a brass metal identification tag attached near the top with two small nails. Printed upon it, 'Joseph Bates Noble's Cane' (first line) and 'Made from Oak Casket of Prophet Joseph Smith' (second line).[4]

Lamar Noble great-grandson to Joseph Bates Noble speaks out, "My great-grandfather Bates Noble served as a bodyguard to the Prophet Joseph Smith; he also was an officer in the Nauvoo Legion. One mission was to rescue the bodies of Joseph and Hyrum Smith from Carthage to Nauvoo. After the rescue Emma Smith, wife of the prophet, allowed each guard a piece of the casket lid for a walking stick in remembrance to their Prophet and General. Joseph Bates Noble elected to keep his stick as you see it today."[5]

As the author, my research found two other references to a casket cane or oak staff. In the book 'Emma', page 119, it states, "Wilford Woodruff was one who had called on Emma prior to leaving for the West. Upon his visit to the Mansion House, Emma had been so touched that she had given him a piece of oak for a staff. It was not just any piece of wood, but a piece of oak Emma had taken from Joseph's coffin. She had also presented Woodruff with a pair of white cotton gloves and a handkerchief for his wife."[6]

In the Deseret News, 1914, an editor, Steven G. Barnett, had written an interesting article entitled "The Canes of the Martyrdom".

Quote, *"Shortly after the martyrdom of the Prophet Joseph Smith in 1844, unusual mementos in his memory – wooden canes – were fashioned from the oak planks of the rough-hewn coffin in which the body was returned to Nauvoo."*

He goes on to say, *"The canes themselves were given to a small group of the Prophet's friends. We do know that Willard Richards, Heber C. Kimball, Dimick Huntington, Wilford Woodruff, and probably Brigham Young had such canes. Today, the only authenticated Martyrdom cane carved from the wood of the oak coffins of Carthage known to exist is that of Dimick Huntington. Perhaps those belonging to Heber C. Kimball and Perrigrine Sessions are also in existence."*

Steven G. Barnett goes on to describe in detail the 'Huntington Cane'. *"The Huntington cane is 33-1/2 inches long, made from medium brown oak, with a hollowed knob handle containing a lock of Joseph Smith's hair. Originally a piece of glass (from the viewing screen of the coffin in which Joseph Smith was laid in state) covered the hole in the knob, having been affixed to a metal guard just inside the top of the cane, but this metal guard has since been broken. The glass is intact, however, still covering the hair it was meant to protect at the base of the knob's hollowed inside. Just below the knob, there is also a band of metal on the shaft, as well as a metal tip at the base of the cane."*[7]

In the Life of Heber C. Kimball by Orson F. Whitney, Heber C. Kimball is quoted as testifying to the healing virtues of these canes:

"How much would you give for even a cane that Father Abraham had used, or a coat or ring that the Savior had worn? The rough oak boxes in which the bodies of Joseph and Hyrum were brought from Carthage, were made into canes and other articles. I have a cane made from the plank of one of those boxes, so has Brother Brigham and a great many others, and we prize them highly and esteem them a great blessing. I want to carefully preserve my cane, and when I am done with it here I shall hand it down to my heir, with instructions to him to do the same. And the day will come when there will be multitudes who will be healed and blessed through the instrumentality of those canes, and the devil cannot overcome those who have them, in consequence of their faith and confidence in the virtues connected with them.

Further on in the same speech, Heber C. Kimball is quoted as saying: "Dr. Richards used to lay his old black cane on a person's head and that person has been healed through its instrumentality, by the power of God." [8]

April 2008, I made a visit to the Daughters of the Utah Pioneers Memorial Museum (DUP Museum); it faces west from the Utah State Capitol building. One could spend hours – what a wonderful place to view relics, pioneer pictures with beautiful frames, and all sorts of early day pioneer things. Walking around suddenly I saw Joseph Bates Noble and his wife Loretta Mecham staring at me. Two individual oil paintings going back to around 1880 more than likely painted in Salt Lake City. Bates Noble was clean shaven with both in their best attire. I could feel their spirit almost like they were speaking out to me saying continue this book. 'It will add spiritual strength to the Noble family and added light into a dark world.'

Located on the third floor of the DUP Museum is the cane display. In viewing this case my eyes centered on one particular black walking cane. I could feel the spirit radiating out from this black cane; the ivory knob seemed to speak out to me saying, 'Brother Noble's oak

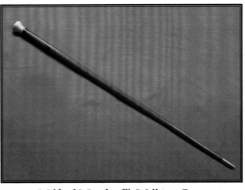

Wilford Woodruff's Walking Cane

stick is a part of me, we bear witness to each other of our authenticity; our mission is in giving honor this day and a past day to which we together protected a Holy Prophet of God and his return home in honor'.

The Museum computer printout stated the following: 'Accession date 1/1/1920, Doners unknown, maker unknown, CIRCA 1840, Classification Canes – Walking Sticks, Description: Cane, painted black, hair in the center of ivory knob, braided locks of Joseph and Hyrum Smith. Possibly coffin cane, made from first coffins Joseph and Hyrum were placed in before moving them to their final ones."[9]

The black cane is six inches shorter in length than Bates Noble's cane stick. However it would be just within a fraction of an inch as square from top to bottom if it had not been sanded round and sloping it gradually from head to tip and placing a metal covering over the tip. It was designed for a short man and one of importance. It is truly a holy cane.

Located on the first floor of the Museum is the "Wilford Woodruff" cabinet display. Two walking canes are located in this glass case. A fancy cane was given to him on his 90th birthday; and the other is a round oak cane approximately the same length and thickness as Bates Nobles' stick. This oak stick was fashioned into a cane with a white knob and a steel tip. The stick was given to him by Emma Smith.[9]

We now have three witnesses speaking out to us, Bates Nobles' oak casket cane, Wilford Woodruff's oak staff, and the black coffin cane located on the third floor of the Pioneer Memorial Museum.

Each cane speaks out, 'The dark deed is done.' A pocket watch owned by John Taylor is dead centered by a pistol ball. Time ends exactly at 5:15 p.m. and twenty-six seconds. The world will never be the same. Two prophets, both brothers, are dead and the news rings around the world. The Latter Day Prophet Joseph Smith and Church Patriarch Hyrum Smith both murdered in cold blood. The date is 27 June 1844.[10]

Suddenly a mob member fires a cannon announcing the death of the prisoners. People are fleeing the City of Carthage in fear, only a few remain to help remove the bodies to the Hamilton Hotel. Taylor's wounds are attended to and Dr. Willard Richards sends a rider by horse in carrying the sad news to Nauvoo.[11]

Not knowing of the murders and around this same time, Samuel the younger brother to Hyrum and Joseph heads out from his home town of Plymouth, and makes his way by horse to warn his brothers of the imminent danger. Mother Lucy shares this experience, "Upon leaving this place of murder, a few of them found my son Samuel coming into Carthage, alone, on horseback, and finding that he was one of our family, they attempted to shoot him. But he escaped out of their hands although they pursued him at top speed for more than two hours.[12]

Samuel out rides his pursuants fleeing for his life. Upon returning home he picks up a fresh horse from a friend and immediately hits the saddle, rides back, and heads into Carthage. The town is now somewhat peaceful, calm, and with a silent stillness as if a light is upon all that remain. The mob executors have fled. Heartbroken, Samuel assists John Taylor in mending his wounds and helps Doctor Richards and others in preparing his brothers' bodies for their return home.[13]

NOTES:

1. The Oak Tree of the Greenwood by Glennie Kindred, Published at Beltane, 1988, p. 1

2. Premium Shaped Casket in Oak by Trappist Caskets, http://www.trappistcaskets.com

3. Cover page – The Oak Tree of Greenwood by Gleannie Kindred, Published at Beltane, 1988.

4. Casket cane stick from the coffin lid of Joseph Smith's casket and given to Bishop Noble by the wife of the Prophet – Emma – in 1844. Refer to this picture in this chapter.

5. Bates Noble told the story to his son Wallace and showed him the Prophet's sword and casket cane. Wallace shared the same experience with his grandson Lamar Noble sometime in the year 1946 in West Bountiful, Utah. Lamar Noble being my first cousin shared the same with me and my wife.

6. Emma, by Keith and Ann Terry, 1980, p. 119. Mentions the oak staff from the casket of Joseph Smith.   Also, Mathias F. Cowley, Wilford Woodruff, SLC, Utah: Deseret News Press, 1909. pp. 227-228.

7. The Canes of the Martyrdom, by Steven G. Barnett, History of the Church of Jesus Christ of Latter-day Saints, Salt Lake City: Deseret News, 1914.

8. Life of Heber C. Kimball, by Orson F. Whitney, made this quote as testifying to the healing virtues of these canes.

9. Pioneer Memorial Museum, 300 North Main Street, Salt Lake City, Utah; Case 3C02, 3rd Floor, Class: 060804 – Canes, Walking Sticks. Accession #: 00651-001, Accession Date: 1/1/1920. Black coffin cane.

10. Comprehensive History of the Church by B. H. Roberts, Vol. II, 1965, pp. 286-291. Shows picture of watch.

11. Ibid, pp. 289-290.

12. History of Joseph Smith by His Mother Lucy Mack Smith, 1945, p. 324

13. Hyrum Smith by Pearson H. Corbett, 1963, pp. 426-427.

DO IT IN HONOR RESCUE THE BODIES

13

A Prophet of God is murdered along with his brother Hyrum the Church Patriarch. Two bodies to rescue. Question, how do you rescue the bodies with honor? Several church historians share different opinions, yet in my search for truth it is apparent each vary - contrary with each other. Only a hidden casket cane made from the lid belonging to Joseph's oak casket opens the door to truth.

Comparing biblical times to that of Joseph Smith – what is the difference? Joseph in biblical times went up to bury his father. Father Jacob was a great prophet and honor was given unto him. In the book of Genesis Chapter 50 verse 9, it states, *"And there went up with him both chariots and horsemen; and it was a very great company."*[1]

Let's look at several opinions as to this rescue, one historian states that the bodies of Joseph and Hyrum were placed in crude boxes and transported by wagon to Nauvoo.[2] Another mentions, two flat bed wagons bearing the bodies being covered with several tree branches for shade and a buffalo hide to keep the flies away.[3] Another states, the martyrs bodies were placed into two wooden boxes covered with prairie grass and flung over with an Indian blanket.[4]

An excellent movie "Praise to the Man" in our personal library shows two flat bed wagons carrying the bodies of Joseph and Hyrum. The bodies are unboxed with their booted feet visible from the tailgate and covered with tree branches to protect each from the heat of the day.[5]

Back to Nauvoo, soon a rider being extremely tired enters into the city. It's nearing midnight on Thursday, June 27th. He makes his way onto the main street towards the Smith house. He crosses paths with Porter Rockwell and the important message is passed on, soon the stillness of the late night at the Smith's home is shattered by a shrill, high-pitched voice at the entry to the dooryard, "They killed them! They killed Joseph and Hyrum!"[6] What mind cannot imagine the horror and anguish that swept over Emma at this time and moment.

Shortly a knock at the Noble house and a door opens quickly. Bishop Noble greets his friend Porter Rockwell sharing the news. This was not unexpected as the spirit had previously touched Bates and his heart is heavy.

Both men spring into action with no hesitation and shortly plans are made for a rescue of the bodies. Around 1:00 a.m. the two officers, Bates and Porter, team up two flat bed wagons, load up two exquisite oak caskets, cover each with a colorful Indian blanket. At approximately 2:00 a.m. they meet with their Nauvoo Legion commander and follow his orders.[7]

Just a reminder, Bates Noble holds the rank of major, Porter as a captain and both men are officers in the Nauvoo Legion. Joseph Smith was their commander and addressed as Lt. General Joseph Smith. Things have changed with the murders and now Col. Jonathan Dunham is addressed as their commander.[8]

Six other officers volunteer to assist Maj. Noble in the rescue attempt. Each are dressed in full uniform, legion swords attached to their sides, heavily armed with pistols, and musket rifles. These men are considered the best officers in the Legion and men of courage. All are bodyguards to the prophet. Each one served in Zion's Camp and shared the experience fighting cholera. These soldiers are going to make sure their leader Lt. General Joseph Smith and Maj. General Hyrum Smith's bodies are returned home in honor and not just with their boots hanging out the tailgate of a wagon.[9]

The road between Nauvoo and Carthage is eighteen miles. It will be in the dark of night with sunrise just four hours away. The road is somewhat dusty, nevertheless a partial moon lights the way. Six hours is allowed in making the journey with arrival time around 8:00 a.m.

Maj. Noble teams the lead wagon with the second body wagon close behind. Six rescue officers with saddle and horse split between the rear and front. The roadway to Carthage is very dangerous – with several hundred mob militia sporting for the head of the Prophet Joseph Smith. The reward is high, $1,000 for the head of the Mormon Prophet.[10]

$1,000 is a large sum of money for those days. Let's put it into perspective. A miller would have to work four years and two months to earn that amount of money. Bates Noble earned $18.00 per month in 1830 working as a miller in a grain factory.[11]

Mother Lucy Mack Smith states, "The mob had the kindness to allow us the privilege of bringing them home and burying them in Nauvoo, notwithstanding the immense reward which was offered by the Missourians for Joseph's head".[12]

Making good time the rescue convoy reached the outskirts of Carthage around 7:00 a.m. The sun is up, warm rays reflect, and the sky above is clear. The evil has left, mobs are in hiding, and a peace prevails somewhat over the town. Samuel Smith the courageous brother joins the convoy and directs the coffin wagons to the front of the Hamilton Hotel.

Prior to this arrival time, Samuel is the one who helped carry John Taylor across the street and into the Hamilton House. Mr. Hamilton and Dr. Willard Richards assisted him. It was 2:00 a.m. before they could reach out to John and dress his wounds and shortly afterwards remove the bodies of Joseph and Hyrum into the Hamilton Hotel.[13]

The eight rescue guards carefully removed the two oak caskets into the main foyer of the hotel. Samuel assisted in the cleaning of the bodies. Maj. Noble calls the officer bodyguards to attention and the eight men marching carefully place the bodies of Lt. General Joseph Smith and Maj. General Hyrum Smith into the oak caskets. The Nauvoo Legion soldiers cautiously load the coffins into each wagon. The placing of the bodies is done in style and not in haste. Prairie grass gathered along the way is sandwiched between the sides, top and bottom of each casket. A colorful wool Indian blanket woven for a chief is placed lightly over the top of each coffin hiding the grass. The polished oak of each casket is visible from the foot end. Basically, the prairie grass, oak coffin, and wool blanket act as a cooler. Flies have no access to these bodies. They will return home in style or should we say in Military Honor.

Shortly after 8:00 a.m. this solemn procession is making its way out of Carthage in a westward direction. Under the leadership of Maj. Bates Noble it will take seven hours before reaching Mulholland Street, about a mile east of the Nauvoo Temple.[14]

NOTES:

1. Holy Bible, King James Version, Genesis 50:9

2. Hyrum Smith, Patriarch by Pearson H. Corbett, 1963, p. 429 under foot notes.

3. "Emma" by Keith and Ann Terry, 1980, p. 96.

4. "No Man Knows My History" by Fawn M. Brodie, 2nd Edition, 1986, p. 396.

5. DVD film - "Praise to the Man", The Inspired Legacy of the Prophet Joseph Smith by the Living Scriptures.

6. "Emma" by Keith and Ann Terry, 1980, p. 94.

7. Story shared by Lamar Noble, Fall 2007, to the author. Lamar is the great- grandson to Joseph Bates Noble - "Keeper of the Sword".

8. Members of the Nauvoo Legion. Source: John Sweeney, Jr., "A History of the Nauvoo Legion in Illinois" MA Thesis, BYU.   Also, Hyrum Smith, by Pearson H. Corbett, 1963, p. 428.

9. Story shared by Lamar Noble, Fall 2007, to the author. Lamar is the great- grandson to Joseph Bates Noble.

10. History of Joseph Smith by his mother Lucy Mack Smith, 1945, p. 324.

11. Joseph Bates Noble's Journal, Transcript BYU-S, p. 3.

12. History of Joseph Smith by his mother Lucy Mack Smith, 1945, p. 324. Also, No Man Knows My History by Fawn M. Brodie, 2nd Edition, 1985, p. 394. Reference made cutting off the prophet's head.

13. History of the Church, Period 1, Vol. III, by Joseph F. Smith, 1905, p. 368. June 4, 1839, the Prophet's narration of his personal experiences: "A number of men living in Daviess County offered the sum of $1,000 for my scalp".

14. Hyrum Smith by Pearson H. Corbett, 1963, pp. 424-427.

CHARIOTS OF ANGELS AND HORSEMEN

14

The exit is made from the town of Carthage towards Nauvoo. Bates Noble is teaming the lead body wagon and along side is Samuel Smith the prophet's younger brother. The party now consists of eleven men, two wagons, and two bodies.[1]

It's Friday morning, the rising sun from the east seems to reflect off the unsheathed legion swords attached to each bodyguard. Their Legion Army uniforms are somewhat dusty and sweaty reflecting the body rescue trip. All lack sleep, nevertheless the mounted men ride in unison with military style.

Yes, it was a small company going for the rescue; however the return trip into Nauvoo will be just as it was when the Prophet Jacob was honored both with chariots and horsemen. "For his sons carried him into the land of Canaan, and buried him in the cave of the field of Machpelha."[2]

Mother Lucy Smith speaks, "Their bodies were attended home by only two persons, save those that went from this place. These were Brother Willard Richards, and Mr. Hamilton; Brother John Taylor having been shot in prison, and nearly killed stayed on at the Hamilton Hotel.[3]

Joseph Fielding Smith states, "The bodies of the martyred prophets were taken to Nauvoo by Dr. Willard Richards, Samuel H. Smith and a guard of eight soldiers."[4]

Unbeknownst, the City of Nauvoo is buzzing like a bee hive preparing a welcome home. The two prophets will return in honor and a stamp will be made into the history of time.

Under the direction of Col. Jonathan Dunham, fifteen hundred Nauvoo Legion soldiers mounted on military decorated horses, sheathe swords attached, full uniform, are making their way east in meeting up with the rescue company. Yes, the bodies will return with chariots of angels and horsemen.[5]

Soon, this small cortege from Carthage is inching its way in and around thousands of people waiting to give honor as they make their way towards the Mansion House. The lead wagon driver passes the reins over to Samuel Smith. Samuel being sick most of the way is now up to the task of guiding the casket wagons.[6]

The Nauvoo Mansion

The home of the Prophet Joseph Smith at the time of the martyrdom.

The coffin wagons park along side facing the Mansion House. Thousands gather to hear Willard Richards speak. He speaks out standing on top a wood frame platform facing the crowd. He addresses the details leading up to the death scene and long enough to calm the gathered saints. Many were embittered with the whole tragic affair. His closing remarks ended asking the people to go home quietly and peaceful to which they did.[7]

Later into the night, Samuel visits with his mother Lucy to ponder upon the calamities now upon the Smith family. He said, "Mother, I have had a dreadful distress in my side ever since I was chased by the mob, and I think I have received some injury which is going to make me sick."[8]

Just fifteen days from this time, Samuel Smith's spirit forsook its earthly body and on July 13, 1844 went to join his brothers and the ancient martyrs in the Paradise of God.[9]

In Nauvoo days, all funerals were held on Sundays, so sometimes they kept the body for a long time, almost a week. An exception was made for the martyred bodies of Joseph and Hyrum. At seven o'clock Saturday morning their bodies were removed from the oak caskets and placed into two pine wood coffins. Each was covered with black velvet fastened with brass nails and lined with white cambrie.[10]

At 8:00 a.m. the Mansion House entry room was opened so that the saints could view the bodies. Bates Noble and other bodyguards were placed in and around the Mansion House and grounds. It is estimated that over ten thousand persons visited the remains on this day. They entered at the west door and left by the north door and the doors closed at 5:00 p.m.[11]

Quickly the pine coffins are switched with the oak caskets. It's time for a mock funeral. Previously sand bags were placed into the oak coffins with the same approximate weight of each man. The upper casket lid is removed from Joseph Smith's oak casket and set aside. Black velvet is fastened across the top face of each with brass nails.[12]

Maj. Noble, Capt. Rockwell, and other legion officers carefully carry the oak caskets out the west door of the Mansion House into the funeral hearses. The two oak caskets leave Joseph's house in honor making their way towards the city graveyard.

Several thousand people are in waiting as they gather for the usual ceremonies. The oak coffins are deposited into a dug grave and buried. One may ask, why the mock funeral? A simple answer, it was to prevent mob enemies from getting possession and cutting off the head of the prophet. Many enemies to the Church thirst for the $1,000 reward.

Around midnight the pine coffins containing the bodies were taken from the Mansion House and carried through the garden, around by the pump, to the Nauvoo House and buried there.[13]

Several months later at Emma's request the caskets were removed and reburied in unmarked graves near the Smith's original Nauvoo homestead on the banks of the Mississippi. A bee house was moved to cover the graves.[14] In 1928, he was re-interred near the original graves with Hyrum on his left and Emma on his right.[15]

NOTES:

1. Essentials in Church History, by Joseph Fielding Smith, 16th Edition, 1960, p. 384. Also, History of Joseph Smith, by his mother Lucy Mack Smith, 1945, p. 324.

2. Holy Bible, King James Version, Genesis 50:13.

3. History of Joseph Smith, by his mother Lucy Mack Smith, 1945, p. 324.

4. Essentials in Church History, by Joseph Fielding Smith, 16th Edition, 1960, p. 384.

5. Hyrum Smith Patriarch, by Pearson H. Corbett, Deseret Book Company, 1976, p. 428.

6. Essentials in Church History, by Joseph Fielding Smith, 16th Edition, 1960, p. 384. Also, Emma by Keith and Ann Terry, 1980, p. 96. This gives reference to Samuel Smith holding the reins. Also, Lamar Noble – gives an account shared by his grandfather Wallace Noble son of Bates Noble.

7. Emma by Keith and Ann Terry, 1980, p. 97. Also – Smith, History of the Church, Vol. VI, pp. 626-628.

8. History of Joseph Smith, by his mother Lucy Mack Smith, 1945, p. 325.

9. Ibid, p. 326.

10. Hyrum Smith Patriarch, by Pearson H. Corbett, Deseret Book Company, 1976, p. 428. Also West Bountiful Pictorial History, by Hugoe and Deppe, 1989, p. 235.

11. Ibid, p. 428 – reference Hyrum Smith.

12. Ibid, pp. 428-429. Also, Emma by Keith and Ann Terry, 1980, p. 99.

13. Ibid, p. 430 – reference Hyrum Smith.

14. Ibid, p. 431 – reference Hyrum Smith.

15. Bitton, George Q. Cannon, 46; Clayton, Journal, June 25, 1844; Leonard, Nauvoo, pp. 400-404; Bernauer, Final Burial," pp. 17-33.

A NEW HOUSE ON WHEELS

15

November 1845 – February 1846, people flocked from all parts of the country into Nauvoo to purchase farms and houses. These were sold extremely low; lower than at a sheriff's auction. For the money; wagons, oxen, horses, cattle and personal articles might be purchased by the Mormons in making their exodus into the west.[1]

The Noble house was located on the main street leading down towards the edge of the river. Bates acquired the building lot in 1841. Shortly afterwards, he built a two story red brick house. The family then moved from Montrose and across the river; soon afterwards he became a Justice of the Peace, cattleman, farmer, builder and Bishop to the Nauvoo L.D.S. 5th Ward.[2]

At this particular time, you might wonder as to why the Prophet's legion sword and casket cane were hid away? Many people in those days thought "Mormonism" would soon end after the deaths of Joseph and Hyrum. To their surprise, the blood of Joseph and Hyrum added new strength within the church. Not long after the murders, the mob militia turned their attention to the destruction of all Mormons. Bishop Noble being fully aware of the impending danger upon his family decided to hide away his relics. His mouth was sealed shut and only his wife knew and shared his story with confidence.

February morning of 1846 was a special day for Mary Adeline as she spent time looking out of her kitchen window; she could see loaded covered wagons, herds of animals, and people heading to the river edge. Each Mormon family waited earnestly to be ferried across the icy river waters.

Two new covered wagons are parked along the south side of her house. Mary Adeline and younger sister Louisa Beman Smith are busy packing flour, corn, wheat, dried vegetables, sea biscuit, warm clothing, heavy bedding, and a few household relics. Louisa reminds her not to forget the foot heaters. Each item is placed neatly into the wagons.

Susan Noble soon returns from visiting a friend. She also helps to load the last few articles into the wagon. A reminder, Susan Noble is the youngest sister to Bates Noble. She spent her growing up years living with Bates and Mary Adeline. It was almost like she was an adopted daughter.

Later in life, Carter E. Grant shares a true story about his grandmother, Susan Noble. "My Grandmother, Susan Noble, who later became the wife of President Jedediah Morgan Grant, was then a happy, black eye miss of fifteen summers. Her brother Joseph Bates Noble, had been one of the bodyguards to the Prophet Joseph Smith, and Susan, as a child, had sat upon the prophet's knee many times and listened with burning interest to the wonderful statements regarding Zion and its future. More than once she had carried secret messages from the Prophet after he had written them and pinned them in the fold of her dress, saying, "Susan, carry this to Hyrum. Guard it with your life."[3]

Susan Noble speaks, "As a young girl, I spent many times in the house of Emma and the Prophet Joseph Smith. One time Joseph's life was in danger and he was desirous in sending a special message to his brother Hyrum. My older brother, Bates, could not leave the Smith home without causing undue suspicion. The Prophet said, 'Susan, I need your help', and stated, 'I need to send a message to my brother, I want you to take it to him. Tell no one where you are going and do not seem to be in a hurry. Walk along as you often do but go immediately to my brother and the Lord will take care of you'. Upon returning Joseph Smith placed his hands upon my head and said, 'Here is a girl who can always be trusted.'"[4]

Bishop Noble returns home from tending to a need within his church calling. While the sisters are visiting in the kitchen, he secretly and carefully removes the sword and casket cane from underneath the stairway; wrapping each and placing them into a side cover of their new house on wheels.

Next he hitches up the horse carriage and makes his way up a busy street to visit the Prophet's mother, Lucy Mack Smith. He is carrying in his pocket a deed to the two story red brick house. Mother Lucy answers the knock; her face brightens up seeing Bishop Noble. They visit and tears flow in parting, Brother Noble passes the deed into her frail hand, it is a gift from him and wife Mary Adeline. Exiting the front door, Bishop Noble tips his hat to the Prophet's mother.[5]

The Noble family is soon on their way into a journey to which they will never return. The brick houses, farms, old friends and the beautiful city of Nauvoo will soon be just a lingering memory. Twelve thousand people crossing the river with thirty thousand cattle, mules, horses and great flocks of sheep, their three thousand wagons make them a fleeing multitude; each crossing upon a journey into the undulating prairie of Iowa. It was the most dramatic emigration of a body of people that had ever occurred in the history of our country.

NOTES:

1. Ford's History of Illinois, p. 412. Also, A Comprehensive History of the Church, by B. H. Roberts, Vol. II, 1965, p. 536.

2. "The Noble – Smith Home", a publication of Nauvoo Restoration, Inc., P. O. Box 215, Nauvoo, Illinois 62354, p. 30.

3. West Bountiful. 1848-1988, A Pictorial History, by LaRue Hugoe – Edith Deppe, 1989, pp. 27-28.

4. Ibid, pp. 27-28.

5. This Week in Church History: Bishop Noble – Friend of the Prophet, by Arnold Irvine, Week Ending January 15, 1966.

TRUE CHARACTER OF BATES NOBLE

16

The first campsite for the Noble's was Sugar Creek just nine miles from Nauvoo City. The advanced wagon companies were to rendezvous for a short period giving time for the catch up wagons and families. The wooded area along the creek lessened somewhat the "bite" of the bitter north wind. The thermometer registered below zero. The ground was frozen and snow covered.

At their new campsite, the snow was soon cleared away and huge fires built in the open spaces. Bates Noble and family joined in with others huddled around the camp fires warming their numbed hands and feet. Favorite hymns soon filled the air and all heads were bowed in prayer to their Father in Heaven whom these exiles had put their trust and keeping. They were now free from the tyranny of mob rule and a determination to build a new Zion in the heart of the mighty Rocky Mountains.

Soon temporary camps were made across Iowa for the purpose of assisting those who were to follow and to permit broken families to recuperate. A few thousand Mormons elected to remain at Nauvoo and surrounding areas another year before heading west. Others headed out in different directions across the country for protection of life and property.[1]

Making their way into Winter Quarters and noting as such, the United States had declared war upon Mexico in June 1846. The fleeing Mormons were asked to provide a battalion of young men to go in defense of their country. Capt. James Allen with his militia caught up with our wagon trails and spoke words with Brigham Young. He called out for one thousand Mormon soldiers. However Brigham through negotiations cut it down to five hundred young men. Brigham asked Bishop Noble and other company leaders to assist in selecting the most able and fit men for this battalion. At the time, the wagon team companies were strung out some one hundred fifty miles between Nauvoo, Council Bluffs and Winter Quarters. Brigham turned facing Capt. Allen and said, "You shall have your battalion."[2]

The loss of five hundred able bodied men necessitated a change of plans causing their leader to locate a temporary camp just opposite Council Bluffs on the Missouri River known as "Winter Quarters". Bishop Noble being a company leader moved his group into Winter Quarters. They built a great log encampment, a grist mill, school houses, and temporary meeting places. By early autumn 1846, the population grew to well over twelve thousand Mormons.

1843-1846 in church history some men did practice plural marriage. At the time it was not considered illegal in the United States and yes, Bates Noble did support more than one family. Special circumstances existed during these extremely hard times. The women in the church out numbered the men and many sisters had already lost husbands and children. Single women as converts traveled from Europe to join up with the Saints.

At Winter Quarters Bates was supporting three families. Going back in time, Bishop Noble with Mary Adeline's approval married a second wife by the name of Sarah B. Alley. The two were married on April 5, 1843 in Nauvoo, Illinois. Sarah was twenty four and Bates thirty three.[3]

Sarah was the daughter of John and Marcy Buffum Alley. She was the eleventh child in a family of thirteen children. She was born October 17, 1819 in Lynn, Essex County, Massachusetts. The family joined the church and moved to Nauvoo. She was taught the gospel and baptized by the Prophet Joseph Smith. She was the first plural wife of Bishop Noble. They were blessed with one son George Omner Noble. George had the distinction of being the first child born of a polygamous union in this dispensation.[4]

Bishop Noble followed church doctrine for this time period and in so doing married a third wife named Mary Ann Washburn on June 28, 1843 in Nauvoo, Illinois. Approval was consented by Mary Adeline and Sarah Noble.[5]

A brief note regarding Mary Ann. Over the years they were blessed with five children, sadly, four of the five children passed away before age eight. One son lived bearing the name of his father grew into manhood with a full life. A young daughter, Mary Elizabeth, died somewhere along the trek westward near Nebraska.

Over a time span of ninety years, Bates shared sixty-six of those years as a devoted husband, father, grandfather and great grandfather. His sweetheart Mary Adeline shared seventeen of those years as a devoted wife and mother. She died on February 16, 1851 in Salt Lake City. She was forty-one and left behind three living children. Six out of nine were buried between Kirtland, Ohio and the Salt Lake valley. All six died before reaching age eight.

Shortly after setting up house in Winter Quarters, Sarah Noble became extremely ill from the hard journey and died in the arms of her husband Bates. It was a short life at age twenty seven. On this cold extremely sad day Bishop Noble and family members gathered as he dug the grave into the frozen ground. He made a name marker out of wood and covered the shallow grave the best he could. Sarah was buried on top of a beautiful hill overlooking the course of the mighty

Missouri River. Here in this silent spot some six hundred other graves were made during these trying months at Winter Quarters.[6]

Neal A. Maxwell said concerning personal suffering, "If we are serious about our discipleship, Jesus will eventually request each of us to do those very things which are most difficult for us to do... Sometimes the best people have the worst experiences, because they are the most ready to learn. The submission of one's will is really the only uniquely personal thing we have to place on God's altar. The many other things we "give," brothers and sisters, are actually the things He has already given or loaned to us. However, when you and I finally submit ourselves by letting our individual wills be swallowed up in God's will, then we are really giving something to Him! It is the only possession which is truly ours to give!"[7]

Five weeks after the graveside funeral for Sarah Noble, Bates married Susan Hammond Ashby on February 1, 1847 at Winter Quarters. She was a friend of the Noble family and traveling in the same wagon train. One reading this story may ask, just who is this Susan Hammond and why the rush?

In Marblehead, Massachusetts lived the family of Edward and Rebecca Flack Hammond. One of the children of this family was a daughter named Susan. The ancestors of Susan had been among the earliest settlers of Maine. Her family had given her a fine heritage.

Susan met and married Nathaniel Ashby and became the parents of a large family. Soon two Mormon missionaries were knocking on their door. Elder Erastus Snow and his companion were laboring in the Eastern States when the door was opened to them. Susan and Nathaniel listened to their message, read the Book of Mormon, prayed for an answer, joined the Church and moved to Nauvoo in 1843.

A son, Benjamin, later in life related this story. "I didn't lack for playmates with twelve brothers and sisters. My dad was a shoe maker and sold his shop in Salem, loaded our family into a rail car to Albany,

New York, by Erie Canal to Buffalo, by steamboat to Cleveland, Ohio and then down the Ohio River into Mississippi and off to the beautiful City of Nauvoo."

"Dad and Mother moved our family into a small log cabin belonging to Bates Noble for six months before moving us into our own house in January 1844. We lived near the house of Joseph Smith. Dad opened up a shoe maker shop facing the main dirt road leading towards the town of Carthage. Nathaniel was considered the best shoe maker in Nauvoo and many visited our shop. One day working with my dad, I can still remember seeing the Prophet Joseph Smith and group on mounted horses making their way down the road towards Carthage. The Prophet stopped and spoke with my dad. "[8] The shoemaker sold a lot of boots that day.

Benjamin continues, "My parents were very active in providing substance in building the Nauvoo Temple. Mother wove two rugs, one with a wreath of roses and another one with a basket of flowers. These together with a beautiful Brussels carpet went into the Temple."[9]

The Nauvoo Temple in the mid-1840s. The temple was burned in 1848 after the Saints were forced to leave Nauvoo and some of the walls were later destroyed by a tornado, leaving the remaining walls so weakened that they had to be razed.

Happy times soon changed for the Ashby family along with many other saints. The Prophet and his brother Hyrum were murdered. Their wooden coffins passed by the Shoe Maker shop. The mobs came into Nauvoo and torched the city along with the Shoe Maker shop. Quoting Benjamin Ashby, "This forced our large family with little preparation out into the cold of winter and across the river. The hard labors of our new house and farm were soon turned into a passing memory. Dad put a lot of effort for such short notice in getting our family across the river and making our way towards Winter Quarters. This stress was too much and he died on the plains near Bonaparte, Iowa".[10]

The Ashby family continued their trek encountering many hardships as they made their way into Winter Quarters. Can anyone imagine the circumstances to which this family was under having to bury their father in a shallow grave midway and just a few short days from the burning city of Nauvoo? Lack of food, lack of shelter, lack of winter clothes and headed into an unknown wilderness with unfriendly Indians.

Bishop Noble's heart went out to this family. Tears were shed along with many personal prayers asking for guidance. After all, he was a special friend to the shoe maker, Nathaniel Ashby, and he was there to share his labors with this family. Bates being a provider and not a slacker, was there at the right time and one must ask how many men in this time and age would take on an additional family with thirteen children. To me as the writer it shows the true character of Bishop Noble and his feelings toward others.

Early spring 1847 thirteen Mormon companies started leaving Winter Quarters in sequence allowing different time schedules for travel. Brigham's company was the first to leave arriving in the Salt Lake valley on July 24th. Bates Noble's company, consisting of one hundred and seventy one pioneers, was followed by the W. Snow and Jedediah M. Grant companies. Bates' company followed a long stretch of wilderness covering some five hundred miles sandwiched between Winter Quarters and Laramie, Wyoming.[11]

The trip by wagon with oxen, cattle, cows, sheep and chickens for these companies was not easy. Many people were sick and many died. Graves were dug and covered. The route along the Platte River was devoid of vegetation. One must remember several weeks ahead ten other companies used the same trail. Bates' company cut up cottonwoods for their horses to browse upon; and at the last lap they were obligated to give up their own scanty stores of grain, flour and biscuits to their weakened animals.

They made their way up and down the rough and jagged foothills. Along the way deer, jack rabbits and fish were added to their very lean diet. Mountain trout were occasionally taken as a treat of sort out of the small crystal clear creeks near the Rocky Mountains.

Late September 1847, Bates Noble's company reached the Echo Canyon slope, halted to rest the wagon teams and mend broken wheels. The vastness of the Rocky Mountains was breath taking and a new dream was soon to come upon them. It was now only a short two day journey and with excitement ahead they made their way up through the ravines and suddenly plunging down out of a canyon's mouth opening up into the barrenness of a huge wide valley.

Before Bishop Nobles' eyes laid the long stretch of land sweeping up to the foothills of the Rocky Mountains. Merging into the western horizon lay the placid waters of the Great Salt Lake, dotted here and there with islands that reared their rocky heads out of the salt water. What a grand sight this was to Bates and company.

His heart pounded as he remembered the words of the ancient Hebrew Prophet, Isaiah, ringing in his ears with a new meaning. Here their new leader Brigham Young had spoken these words, "This is the right place" and in the immediate years ahead as they put their hands to the plow a complete fulfillment of these ancient spoken words and modern prediction would be made. The valley shall blossom as a rose and a great temple to the Lord Jesus Christ shall be built as viewed by that ancient prophet.[12]

NOTES:

1. West Bountiful. 1848-1988, A Pictorial History, by LaRue Hugoe – Edit Deppe, 1989, p. 28.

2. A Comprehensive History of the Church, Century One, Vol. VI, by B. H. Roberts, 1965, pp. 60-121.

3. Documentary History of the Church, Vol. 5, p. 385. Sarah Alley became the first plural wife of J. B. Noble.

4. "A Nobleman in Israel" – Joseph Bates Noble, Their Child – George Omner, by Hazel Noble Boyack.

5. Mary Ann Washburn Noble Whiting, by her granddaughter, Gwenevere Miner Hickman.

6. Documentary History of the Church, Vol. 5, p. 385.

7. Neal A. Maxwell, Talk: Concerning Personal Suffering, Conference Report, October 1995, p. 30.

8. West Bountiful. 1848-1988, A Pictorial History, by LaRue Hugoe – Edit Deppe, 1989, p. 24.

9. Ibid.

10. Benjamin Ashby, copy of holograph, BYU-S, pp.9-10.

11. Essentials in Church History, by Joseph Fielding Smith, 1950, Route of Travel, pp. 439-440. Also, Noble Company arrived in October 1847, p. 461.

12. Ibid, p. 450.

FOOTPRINTS OF THE PAST

17

The Bates Noble Company 171 strong emerged into the vast Salt Lake valley and before their eyes laid the long stretch of land sweeping up to the foothills of the Rocky Mountains.[1]

Wrapped and hidden away were his two legion swords and a casket cane. The trusted cap and ball musket rifle was attached to the side of the Noble wagon. The Legion Sword of Joseph Smith and his own personal sword were two of his most prized possessions.

Exploration of the surrounding valley commenced right after the Noble Company entered into the Salt Lake basin. In the fall of 1847, Bates Noble, Samuel Parrish, James Adams, Perrigrine Sessions, and a

few other Mormons moved into the valley north (Davis County) with a few head of cattle. Summer 1849 William Reed Smith arrived with the Austin Grant Company went north and joined up with the Parrish family. The towns at the foot of the mountain included Farmington, Parrish Creek and Bountiful. Parrish Creek was later named Centerville being the center between Farmington and Bountiful. The first winter was spent living in their covered wagons and the following winter in their huts.[2]

Bates Noble headed north on horseback exploring the Great Basin. He liked the area and the soil. He tracked back and forth across Farmington, Parrish Creek and Bountiful. The settlements at this time were close to the foothills of the Rocky Mountains. No one was interested in land to the west near the Great Salt Lake other than a few Indians.

After checking out the area, he came across a crystal clear creek of cold water flowing out of the base of the mountains weaving its way across the valley somewhat northwest several miles eventually entering into the swamps of the Great Salt Lake. Native trout were darting and swimming and hiding as the shadow of his pack horse and body followed the outline of the creek. The small stream made a bend northwest in direction and later in years the creek bend became known as 1000 North and Onion Street in West Bountiful.

Bates Noble and wife Sylvia Loretta Mecham were married in January 1857 in Salt Lake City, Utah. Loretta's nickname was "Rettie" and she earned the name at age fourteen living at Council Bluffs. She helped her father build a log house, plant crops, and tend traps as he was a trapper as well as a farmer. She did not like the snakes in tending traps along the river banks.[3]

Bates was a Big Man in spirit. His new wife Loretta though younger by twenty-eight years brought new life into the Big Man. It takes a Big

Man to be the Keeper of the Prophet's Sword. He was rough on the edges and now is polished like a rock in the bed of a stream.

The two returned to the bend in the creek and built a two room adobe house. Behind his adobe home he built a barn with a small hay loft for his prize horses. They uprooted the sagebrush, dug up the black willows and with a team of horses turned the black rich loamy soil. Bates knew the family could plant and harvest.

Gray and white seagulls proved to be their friends by eating the yellow grass hoppers and crickets sharing their garden. It was the beginning of West Bountiful and later as a town.[4]

The harvest was plentiful with large orange carrots, yellow onions, brown potatoes, red tomatoes, purple eggplant, white celery, green peppers and all from the rich black soil and water in the creek. The air was pure and the summer sunshine was abundant.

Bates and Loretta later added to the house on the front side. This house stood for nearly one hundred years; however, due to age was torn down and replaced with another house. The Noble house was built upon ancient Indian ground not too far from the shoreline of the Great Salt Lake. It was one of the first pioneer houses in this area.

The Noble's lived a happy life on their small farm. It was one of thrift with many varieties of fruit and vegetables. One year, Bates was awarded a cider mill as a prize for the greatest variety of fruits and vegetables grown. Hundreds of gallons of vinegar were produced along with a molasses mill producing several hundred gallons of dark molasses.[5]

Loretta was an expert in making clothing from sheep wool; she knew how to use a cradle in harvesting wheat and threshed it with a club. She could make a whole sock for Bates while traveling from West Bountiful to Salt Lake City by ox team. "Rettie" was a hard worker, devoted, prayerful wife and mother, and was noted as an excellent cook. What more could Bates ask for, a devoted wife and an excellent cook.[6]

My growing up years taught me much regarding this old adobe house. I worked on the farm along with my cousin Lamar, he being like an older brother to me and I like a younger brother to him. His dad and mother were like a second set of parents to me. Aunt Bernice is a sister to my father. Our house was located directly across the street from the old Noble home. Lamar's house set west just a few feet separated by a dirt driveway with large trees.

Those days many ring neck pheasants frequented the farm. Sometime in the early 1950's we were working the ground on the north end and spotted several large ring necks. Lamar taught me a lesson of accuracy using a hole file. We slowly approached several pheasants hiding within a vegetable flowage. They suddenly flew up into the sunny sky directly above us with great speed and before I knew it Lamar threw his file into the summer air nailing a ring neck on the bottom side. To our surprise the pheasant dropped like a rock with the bird ending up in the frying pan later that day.[7]

Those footprints left on this day fell upon a rich soil covering many foot prints of a great pioneer, Joseph Bates Noble. He had worked this farm one hundred years earlier with his son William Wallace. Wallace followed the footprints in the soil with his son Delbert. Lamar, his son, to whom I now speak, was working the farm this hot summer day with me. This story is dedicated to the footprints of father-to-son covering one hundred years.

The barn stood until 2007 outlasting the family adobe house. The horses were some of the best in the Bountiful community. The Noble family wove their own cloth and sewed their own clothing. It was a very industrious family.[8]

Time just seems to roll along almost like a dream and the present is much different than the year the old adobe house was first built. It stood out as the sunset closed the day across the Great Salt Lake covering the sagebrush area of Bountiful with darkness of night. Early each day, Bates was out cultivating the thirty acre plot with his team of horses, planting the seed and directing the creek water with irrigation ditches.

Time passed into the 1880's with the Noble family welcoming new families into the area. Their houses were much different being built out of brick carried in by wagon teams out of Salt Lake City. The large red brick mansions grew up and down the dusty dirt road later to be called "Onion Street". Two story brick carriage houses were built to match the new neighborhood houses. Horse stables were apart of each along with a hay loft on the second story. The plot was approximately ten acres for pasture and garden. Many raised yellow onions to sell at the market. This town now consisted of new Mormon pioneers, houses dotting the street, trees planted, flowers growing, children playing, men and children working the farms, and truly a town of beauty.[9]

Around 1886, a new Mormon chapel was built for worship along with a cultural hall. This brick building was used for plays, dances and social gatherings. Sunday was a day of rest from labor with many neighbors gathered for services. Neighbors were considered as brothers and sisters in the gospel, all were thought of as family each looking after the needs of neighborhood children and truly a happy time to live.[10]

Will Rogers has been quoted as making the following statement regarding small towns. "The small town is passing. We not only ought to regret it, we ought to do something to remedy it. It was the incubator that hatched all our Big Men, and that's why we haven't got as many Big Men today as we used to."[11]

Though small in stature, Joseph Bates Noble was a Big Man.

NOTES:

1. Essentials in Church History, by Joseph Fielding Smith, 16th edition, 1960, p. 461.

2. William Reed Smith - Mormon Pioneer by David F. Smith. Revised version by Howard C. Smith - great grandson, p. 1.

3. Joseph Bates Noble shared this story with his son Wallace Noble. Wallace shared this story with his grandson Lamar Noble, "Keeper of the Sword", and Lamar shared this story with Howard Smith, author of this book, November 2007.

4. Ibid.

5. Ibid.

6. Ibid.

7. The Life and Times of Howard Carlos Smith and His Ancestors, by Howard C. Smith, p. 33.

8. Ibid., pp. 32-33.

9. Ibid., pp. 36-39.

10. West Bountiful, 1848-1988, A Pictorial History, by LaRue Hugoe - Edith Deppe, 1st Edition, 1989, pp. 154-158.

11. Will Rogers - small town statement, West Bountiful - A Pictorial History, by LaRue Hugae and Edith Deppe, 1989, p. 508.

APPENDIX

Provenance
of the Sword

An Account by Howard C. Smith

Uncle Delbert (Del) and Aunt Bernice Smith Noble are two of my favorite people. They were like a second set of parents to me while I was growing up in West Bountiful, Utah. Del and Bernice had two children – Lamar and June.

Del was a produce farmer making a living off of thirty acres or so left to him by his father William Wallace Noble. Wallace and his wife LeNora lived in the old adobe house once belonging to his father Joseph Bates Noble. The house was located on 10th North and 800 West before it was demolished. Lamar and his wife Teri now live upon this location in their house (2009).

1948 is where I came into the picture. My first real job in life was at age seven working on the old Bates Noble farm now belonging to Uncle Del. He taught me how to work at an early age. I can still vividly remember how Uncle Del taught me the trade of weeding yellow onions with a bent steak knife. The rows of onions looked as if they were a mile long. I worked this farm on and off for over ten years. He provided me employment up through my senior year of high school.

My uncle never used cross words or bad language. He paid me in cash and was always honest in his dealings. He was of good character and believed in the Prophet Joseph Smith. In the late 1940's he hired a Mexican family to live on the farm during the summer months in a storage shed that was adapted into living quarters. They were really hard workers and consisted of seven children, a mother, a father and a grandfather. They liked Uncle Del so much that they returned year after year to work the farm. I grew to love this family and their honesty in doing a days work for a days pay.

At age sixteen, in the summer of 1957, Uncle Del sat me down by the old adobe house. He told me about the Prophet Joseph Smith's Nauvoo Legion Sword, pistol and casket stick and his grandfather's ball and cap musket rifle. He shared many stories. He told me the sword belonging to the Prophet was hid away in the adobe house.[1]

An Account by Lamar Noble

"I was born in 1935 to Del and Bernice Noble. My father – my grandfather, Wally Noble, ran the family farm that was originally owned by my great grandfather Joseph Bates Noble. Joseph Bates Noble was an early convert to the Mormon Church, he was a bodyguard to Joseph Smith. He was also a Capt. of fifty, and a Mormon Bishop. In 1841 he performed the first plural marriage in the Church marrying Joseph Smith to Bates' sister-in-law, Louisa Beman."[2]

"Joseph Bates Noble was riding with Joseph Smith to Carthage Jail, when Joseph took him aside and gave him his sword and told him to go back to Nauvoo. After Joseph Smith was killed, Joseph Bates Noble and some other men sneaked his body (which was in a oak box) back to Nauvoo. All the men were given a stick from the box."

"Joseph Bates Noble brought the sword, a ball and cap rifle, and the oak stick across the plains to his adobe home in West Bountiful. Before his death he gave these items to my grandfather Wally. Wally lived in the adobe house until his death in 1956. He gave these items to my father (Del) who in turn gave them to me before his death in 1994. I have tried to keep them safe and maintain them in good condition." [3]

This statement was hand written and signed by Lamar Noble May 27, 2008.

An Account by Arnold Irvine

An article written by Arnold Irvine dated January 15, 1966. It was on the front page in the Church Weekly and titled 'Bishop Noble – Friend of the Prophet'. A pencil picture was also included showing Bates Noble pitching hay with the Prophet.

Arnold Irvine states, "Bishop Joseph Bates Noble rode toward Carthage with his close friend and leader. The Prophet rode off the road with him a short distance. The parting was a sad one. The Prophet gave the Bishop his legion sword as a token of their friendship and asked him to deliver a note to Mrs. Smith. That was the last time Bishop Noble saw the Prophet alive."

Arnold goes on to say, "His love never diminished for the man who had restored the gospel. Hectic days followed, but one of the Bishop's final acts as he was preparing to leave for the west was the delivery of the deed to his house and lot in Nauvoo as a gift to Lucy Smith, the Prophet's mother. This was undoubtedly a gesture of love and loyalty to the Prophet as much as to his mother."

This article also plays tribute to Bishop Noble by stating, "When the Prophet Joseph Smith rode out of Nauvoo toward Carthage on that fateful June morning in 1844, his Bishop was among those who accompanied him. The Bishop was Joseph Bates Noble of the Nauvoo Fifth Ward. The Prophet and the Bishop had been through a kaleidoscope of experiences together in the eleven or so years that they had known each other. Many strands had been woven into the friendship that now bound them together."[4]

An Account by Hazel Noble Boyack

Hazel Noble Boyack a grand daughter to Joseph Bates Noble and daughter of Edward Alvah Noble gives her account. It was written and collected in a binder on September, 1961. The title is "A Nobleman in Israel" and available on the website under its title name. It is an excellent presentation regarding the Noble family. <u>However there are several inconsistencies regarding the whereabouts of her grandfather's legion sword.</u>

On page 16 she states, "He also served as one of the bodyguards to Lt. General Joseph Smith. The sword Sergeant Noble used in this military organization was brought over the plains by him in 1847, and is now in possession of Delbert Noble family of Bountiful, Utah."[5]

On page 17 Hazel continues, "On that fateful day June 1844, when Joseph Smith party left for Carthage, his faithful friend Joseph Bates, rode with them. A few miles out of Nauvoo, Bro. Bates became ill. He and the Prophet rode together into a small ravine near the road. Here Joseph Bates was to part with his beloved leader for the last time. After a parting handclasp, the Prophet gave to him his sword telling him to take it as a token of their friendship."[6]

She mentions that the two legion swords were carried into the Salt Lake Valley in 1847 and the prize relic sword was in Joseph Bates Nobles' life for almost fifty-three years.

Regarding the prize relic sword, she continues, "Shortly before his death in 1900 he presented to his eldest son, Edward Alvah Noble, my father, who in turn gave it to his eldest son, Charles Leslie Noble, Alpine, Arizona. A few years ago the Noble family presented this sword to the Church Museum as a historical relic."[7]

<u>The sword speaks out, "the old Legion Sword of the Prophet Joseph Smith never left the room or the stairway of Bates' adobe house in West Bountiful." Around his 80ᵗʰ birthday, Joseph Bates Noble presented his personal legion sword to his eldest son, Edward Alvah Noble and the ball-cap musket rifle to his son Wallace Noble.</u> Wallace Noble was the son who remained on the farm with his father and after Bates' passing continued to live in the old adobe house with his wife and family.

Wallace Noble is the grandfather to my cousin Lamar Noble. Lamar at the present time is the "Keeper of the Prophet's Sword".

<u>The question to ask, where is Joseph Bates Noble's personal legion sword today?</u> No one knows its whereabouts. March 2008, checking with the Church Museum, no record recorded regarding its donation by the Arizona Noble family; likewise the Daughter of the Utah Pioneer Memorial Museum has no record recorded.

Could it possibly be that Joseph Bates Noble's personal legion sword for some reason or other is hid away and never was donated to the Church? One can only speculate. My research did not provide the answer and hopefully someday Joseph Bates Noble's Legion Sword will appear.

Joseph Bates Noble
Keeper of the Prophet's Sword
24 June 1844 – 17 Aug 1900
Died at age 90

Sylvia Loretta Mecham Noble

William Wallace Noble

Keeper of the Prophet's Sword
17 Aug 1900 – 4 Jan 1956
Died at age 80

Lenora Smith Noble

Delbert Noble

Keeper of the Prophet's Sword
4 Jan 1956 – 30 Apr 1994
Bernice Smith Noble

Lamar Noble

Present Keeper of the Prophet's Sword
Received possession on
30 Apr 1994
Teri Noble

NOTES:

1. An account given by Howard Carlos Smith, Author of this book, Keeper of the Prophet's Sword, June 15, 2008.

2. Joseph F. Smith, Jr., Blood Atonement and the Origin of Plural Marriage Salt Lake City, Utah: The Deseret News Press, p. 75:

LDS Affidavits Support Bennett's Claim

When President Joseph F. Smith of the Mormon Church needed to publish the names of Joseph's alleged wives in order to defend LDS polygamy, he drew on John Bennett's statement about Louisa. He listed the first plural wife as "Louisa Beman, married to the Prophet April 5, 1841, Joseph B. Noble officiating" (*Historical Record 6.233*). This was in agreement with Bennett's statement on page 256 in his book.

In desperate need of defending their position, the leaders of the Mormon Church obtained affidavits from a number of individuals, including Joseph Noble. The LDS record states:

AFFIDAVIT OF JOSEPH BATES NOBLE

Territory of Utah

County of Salt Lake.   ss

Be it remembered that on the 26th day of June, A.D. 1869, personally appeared before me, James Jack, a notary public in and for said county, Joseph Bates Noble, who was by me sworn in due form of law, and upon his oath saith, that on the fifth day of April, A.D. 1841, at the city of Nauvoo, County of Hancock, State of Illinois, he married or sealed Louisa Beaman to Joseph Smith, President of the Church of Jesus Christ of Latter-day Saints, according to the order of celestial marriage revealed to the said Joseph Smith.

Joseph B. Noble.

Subscribed and sworn to

by the said Joseph Bates Noble,

the day and year first above written.

[Seal]

James Jack, Notary Public.

3. An account given by Lamar Noble, great grandson of Joseph Bates Noble, written testimony given May 27, 2008.

4. Special tribute to Bishop Noble given in the Church Weekly, issue date – January 15, 1966, by Arnold Irvine of the Seventy.

5. An account given by Hazel Noble Boyack, September 1961, 'A Nobleman in Israel', pp. 16-17.

6. Ibid., p. 17.

7. Ibid.

APPENDIX

Wives
and Children

A book could be written just about the seven wives of Joseph Bates Noble. This is not my intention, even though it would be a book of much interest. Especially if one had at their finger tips the missing information in the family history.

Around 1860, a blessing was given to Joseph Bates Noble by Church Patriarch John Smith.[1] I have included just a small part:

"Joseph Bates Noble, the Lord has had his eyes upon thee through the lineage of thy fathers. For upwards of 400 years thy fathers have had visions of the coming forth of this work and lived in hopes of seeing it, but have died without the sight."

"Thou shalt also have numerous posterity on the earth. They shall even excel David and Soloman for strength and wisdom."

"Thy name shall be had in honorable remembrance in the church forever."[2]

The Children of Joseph Bates and Mary Adeline Beman Noble

Meriam Noble	Mary Adelia Noble
Joseph Heber Noble	Hirum Brigham Noble
Nephi Noble	Eliza Theodsia Noble

Louisa Noble   Benjamin Noble

Edward Alvah Noble

<u>The Only Child of Joseph Bates and Sarah B. Alley Noble</u>

George Omer Noble

<u>The Children of Joseph Bates and Mary Ann Washburn Noble</u>

Mary Elizabeth Noble   Hyrum Noble

Tamer Noble   Alfred Noble

Joseph Bates Noble, Jr.

<u>The Child of Joseph Bates and Susan Hammond Ashby Noble</u>

Louisa Adeline Noble

<u>Joseph Bates and Millicent London Noble had no children</u>

<u>The Children of Joseph Bates and Julia Rosetta Thurston Noble</u>

Josephine Noble   Sarah Maria Noble

Harriet Noble   Charles Noble

<u>The Children of Joseph Bates and Sylvia Loretta Mecham Noble</u>

Susan Vilate Noble   Frank Mecham Noble

Elnora Noble   Loretta Sylvia Noble

Bates Mecham Noble   William Wallace Noble

Mary Beatrice Noble   Joseph Parley Noble

Erastus Alma Noble   Zina Pearl Noble

Artemesia Noble

The succeeding generations of Joseph Bates Noble's descendants can be found in a compiled volume of family group sheets, available at the Genealogical Office in Salt Lake City, Utah.

NOTES:

1. Essentials in Church History, by Joseph Fielding Smith, 1950, p. 702. John Smith born Sept. 22, 1832 at Kirtland, Ohio; ordained Patriarch to the Church, Feb. 18, 1855 by Brigham Young.

2. A blessing by John Smith, Patriarch, upon the head of Joseph Bates Noble. Blessing located at the Daughter of Utah Pioneers Museum – Manuscript Department under Joseph Bates Noble file.

Index

P

About the Author

Howard Carlos Smith is a native of West Bountiful, Utah. He holds a B.S. Degree in Automotive Engineering from Utah State University and a Master's Degree in Industrial Education from Brigham Young University. He is a research historian in his own family. Many years have been spent as a trainer in industry and a secondary educational teacher. Over 15,000 students have attended his classes spanning a period of forty-five years.

He has served in various church positions. One of the highlights of his life was serving a two year mission throughout Florida and Puerto Rico. He was one of three missionaries to open up the Island of Puerto Rico for the preaching of the Gospel. He has many stories to tell on this topic.

He and his wife, Jolene, share seven children and eight grandchildren. They reside in Burley, Idaho.